Athens

Athens

John Gill

INNERCITIES
Signal Books

First published in 2011 by
Signal Books Limited
36 Minster Road
Oxford OX4 1LY
www.signalbooks.co.uk

A catalogue record for this book is available from the British Library

ISBN 978-1-904955-83-2 Paper

Cover Design: Devdan Sen
Production: Devdan Sen
Cover Images: Valeria Cantone | Dreamstime.com (main photo); backover
    inset – Wikipedia Commons
Photos courtesy of Wikimedia Commons. We would also like to thank
    Manolis Anastasakis, Theo Angelopoulos, Bios, Mikaël Delta, DESTE
    Foundation for Contemporary Art, Apostolos Doxiadis, Les Amis de
    Xenakis, Hollwich Kushner LLC (HWKN) architects, Panos Koutras,
    Yorgos Lanthimos, Dimitris Lyacos, Amanda Michalopoulou, Dimitris
    Papaioannou, Athina Rachel Tsangari and Savina Yannatou.
Printed in India

Contents

Introduction

Athens may share an address with its glorious past, but the city today is largely an invention of the most recent 180 years of that history, roughly the age of the modern Greek state. Most historians regard this period, when they consider it at all, as an addendum or appendix to the main narrative, which for some ended over 2600 years ago with the death of Pericles. For the city's four million inhabitants, of course, those 180 years are the main narrative. It is the period in which Greece invented itself as Greece, with Athens as its new capital; when it founded a constitution, constructed a parliament, wrote a legal system, built its first universities, hospitals, museums, galleries and libraries, and published two contradictory dictionaries of its language. While the ancient architecture and statuary have been there for three thousand years and are not going anywhere any time soon, the city is rapidly accelerating into its future. It is in the spaces between the past, present and future that we find the living Athens.

The opening decades of the twenty-first century are interesting times to be in Athens, not least in the sense of the apocryphal "Chinese" curse parading as a good luck wish. In Athenian chronology, however, if we measure it from the Golden Age of Pericles, this is the city's 26th century, a longevity to which few other cities can lay claim. This leads us inevitably to a paradox: much of its history during those twenty-six centuries is, if not exactly blank, then largely silent, and at one point at least, in the late sixteenth century, Athens disappeared, briefly, off the cultural map of the European landmass altogether. While this book considers the ancient and classical periods, and even dips briefly into geological time, it addresses itself chiefly to those 180 years, and in particular the past half-century of Athenian history and culture.

The last thing the world, or Athens, need is another book about the splendours of ancient Greece. Age, scholarly bias and the tourism industry have made its antiquities the key reason for visiting Athens, usually at the expense of newer cultural phenomena—to highlight a few random examples: the paintings of either its Impressionist or

Cubist schools; its art nouveau and deco architecture and more recent examples of modernism and post-modernism (and this in a city that has yet to acquire a proper skyscraper); generations of world-class writers who have gone untranslated into other languages; an even newer new wave of young filmmakers who are barely out of their teens; an underground music scene that is rewriting the rules of electronica as laid down in Detroit and Düsseldorf. What follows is a primer to this modern, living Athens, and its *raison d'etre* is simple: its author has never found a book that told him about these things and others besides.

This is not to attempt an equivalence between the modern and the ancient, merely to note that a city without a present and a future is a city in danger of becoming a theme park, and Athens is too interesting a city to be abandoned to nostalgia. Athens has, in fact, already experienced two bouts of nostalgia for its own past: around the third century BCE, before there was anywhere else in Europe to be nostalgic about; and in the nineteenth century, when it was gripped by what might be described an early example of post-modern nostalgia and began re-importing its own past—from Germany. Another bout would be three too many.

While some Greek historians have been busy burning bridges with the ancient past—to the extent, for example, of asserting that classical Athenian democracy, such as it was, bears no relation to the modern version—the past has a habit of rebuilding those bridges under cover of darkness. Two current controversies in both Athens and Greece—the status of the sizeable Muslim minority and the treatment of refugees—overlook the historical fact that Athens has been a racially mixed city since its earliest days. The city was probably founded by immigrants (according to Plutarch, no less a founding figure than Themistocles was a foreign upstart) and thrived on the complex patterns of migration and trade across the Mediterranean through the centuries. Its contemporary cultural mix, in which the Muslim community represents less than one of the six per cent resident non-Greeks in a constellation of ethnic groups from Africa, Asia, Eastern and Northern Europe, the Middle East, South America and elsewhere, is probably little different from that at the time when Themistocles thought it would be a good idea to build a surrounding wall to protect the city's cultural mix from the barbarians outside.

Athenian thinkers during those 180 years of its modern history, from nineteenth-century revolutionaries to twenty-first-century queer psychogeographers, have all tussled with a conundrum that has persisted through three millennia: how to retain the best of the past while also embracing the possibilities of the future. Current events in both capital and country may seem to have put the immediate future on hold, but they have twenty-six centuries of the past pressing them into the future, and whatever the short-term may hold, Athens will emerge one way or another. As an unlikely refugee who himself washed up on a beach near Athens in the 1990s, the late Jacques Derrida, wrote, with deliberate ambiguity, "Athens, still remains."

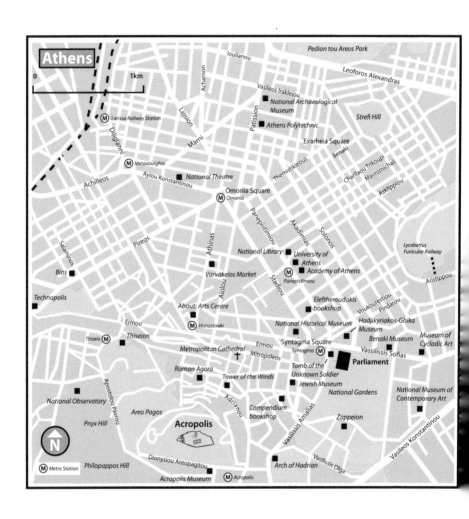

1 | Contours
Geography and History

Athens is defined by the mountains and sea that surround it, and by the tectonic movement and erosion that carved this jumble of low hills in the centre of the Attica Plain. Its central geological feature, the Acropolis or "higher city" (from the Greek *akron*, which can mean higher, top or extremity, and *polis*, city) is, like the hills that surround it, part of a nappe or kippe of limestone, an outcrop of rock formed by tectonic movement, here weathered over the sixty to one hundred million years since the rock formed in the Late Cretaceous period. A nappe, specifically, is a geological feature that has been shunted some way from its original position by tectonic forces. The Acropolis rock actually started out near Mount Hymettus, fifteen miles east of its current position, and is creeping very slowly westwards. In another sixty to one hundred million years, it will be a pretty islet somewhere off Piraeus or Cape Sounion, although by then the tectonic subduction that is causing mainland Greece to sink into the sea may have tugged Athens beneath the waves.

It is these hills that give parts of central Athens, such as modern-day Kolonaki, the appearance of a Mediterranean San Francisco—or, indeed, the steeper parts of Glasgow. In the case of the Acropolis, its modern shape is also due to more recent human engineering, particularly infills of local sandstone and Athens schist, in preparation for the building projects of the Golden Age, which we might date to Pericles' rule between 461 and 429 BCE. Some of this prehistoric landfill, scuffed to a shine by millions of visitors' shoes over the centuries, is over forty feet deep: perhaps a necessary measure to support the fantastic feats of engineering that lofted the huge columns and pediments of the Parthenon temple some 512 feet above sea level and into the sky. While barely half a mountain, on a clear day it offers

Heading west: The Lycabettus Hill is following the Acropolis towards the sunset

views as far as the island of Poros, 35 miles away as the crow flies. So prominent is it from the sea that the city's early navies used to take a sighting on the light glinting off a statue of the goddess Athena on the Acropolis as they navigated their way home.

For most of the eight thousand years that humans have used the Acropolis hill, the Acropolis *was* Athens, and on at least one occasion it was abandoned entirely, only to be re-inhabited later. The earliest archaeological finds around the Acropolis complex have dated its oldest structure, remnants of a large temple dedicated to Athena Polias, protector of the city, to the sixth century BCE. It is likely that the area would have been settled as far back as the Greek Neolithic period before the sixth millennium BCE—the Acropolis rock is pocked with very troglodyte-friendly caves—but as successive occupiers have pointed out through its history, the entire Attica Plain is a very poor choice for either settlement or farmland, with a heavy clay soil and scant natural water. Yet Athens has endured, through periods of glory and abandonment and occupation by most of the armies on the move through the Mediterranean throughout those millennia, largely due to accidents of geopolitics and the excellent protected moorage at its ancient natural harbours of Faleron and, later, nearby Piraeus.

Athens is a landlocked city but one with the sea in its bones—and in its ears. We might also say it has the sea in its heart, and its soul. While it lacks a Hudson, Rhine, Seine or Thames (its two main rivers, the Kifissos and the Ilissos, were lost beneath two centuries of urban construction until recent decades, and it took the building of the new Syntagma station on the Metro system to unearth the dry bed of what was once the Eridanos river), one of its oldest streets, Pireos, promises to get you to the sea just five miles away in as straight a line as possible. (In fact, Pireos follows the route of the ancient Long Walls that once defended the vital link between Athens and its seaport.)

The city, and the country it has represented since 1834, were both founded on sea trade and sea politics thousands of years ago. We can trace these ties to a sea narrative that became a cornerstone of world literature, Homer's *Odyssey*, in addition to the journeys that

3

took Greeks to and from the Trojan Wars in his *Iliad*. Greece has long had a particularly intimate relationship with its surrounding seas: its nearly 82,000 square miles of landmass are edged with a convoluted 10,000 miles of coastline—4,600 of them fringing all those lovely islands. Its interactions with the rest of the Mediterranean, either in peaceable trade or its frequent excursions into aggressive military expansionism, have usually been conducted by sea, as have most movements of trade, population and the communications of a nation reaching out across an archipelago of 247 inhabited islands (of a casual roundup of maybe 6000 largely uninhabited ones).

The sea recurs in the country's mythology, folkways and culture, from Homer's wine-dark variety up to Nobel laureate George Seferis' haikus, and even the poetry of cultish *poète maudit* Kostas Karyotakis, who tried to drown himself in it. The sea is everywhere you go, literally and metaphorically: in the novels of Nikos Kazantzakis and Alexandros Papadiamantis; in the paintings of the great Greek sea painter Constantinos Volanakis and the works of the Greek Impressionists of the nineteenth century; from the music of Manos Hadjidakis and Mikis Theodorakis, through the great *rebetiko* performers to some unlikely corners of post-punk, such as the watery masterpiece *Sixteen Haiku* by the Athens group Sigmatropic (more of which later) and in the films of anyone from Jules Dassin to Theo Angelopoulos, who rarely finishes a movie without taking his camera to the seaside. It even turned up in the opening and closing celebrations of the 2004 Olympics, in the symbolism of renegade dramatist Dimitris Papaioannou and his figure of a little boy aboard a giant paper boat drifting across the temporary sea which Papaioannou installed in the Olympic Stadium. And nowhere is the Greek relationship with the sea more poignant than in the Homeric notion of *nostos*, homecoming, particularly at the start of the great festival of the Greek calendar, *Pasca*, Easter, when Athens goes home to the islands, and the islands go home to Athens.

Perhaps the most surprising fact about the history of Athens is its persistent dwarfism: its contours remained more or less static for the best part of those eight thousand years, and only began to change drastically in the mid-nineteenth century. While each city was shaped by very different circumstances, it is interesting to compare it to London and, particularly, Paris, the city on which the nine-teenth-century "New Athens" modelled itself. To take at random the year 1820, the eve of the War of Independence that was to usher in the modern Greek state, is to find Athens resembling a small rural village with an unusually large archaeological relic attached. In 1820 London already stretched to encompass Kensington in the west and Wapping in the east, with a population of 1.25 million. Paris already had around 700,000 inhabitants filling the twelve central *arrondisse-ments* in the city centre. Yet Athens at the time resembled what one visitor called a "miserable shanty town", comprising the Acropolis and perhaps two hundred buildings used by the occupying Ottoman Turkish garrison and its dependents, with a total population in one estimate of barely four thousand souls. A famous painting from a few years later, Peter von Hess' *The Entry of King Otho of Greece in Athens (*1835), shows a crowd surrounding the new king (on the steps of the Thiseion temple and nothing between it and the Acropolis but open countryside.

This was, admittedly, at one of the frequent low points in the ever-changing population levels of Athens, which at its classical and Roman peaks topped 100,000 inhabitants in the city and its satellite settlements. By 1900 New Athens had a population of around 125,000, although this was already overflowing a newly-built city originally designed for a projected occupancy of, at most, forty thou-sand inhabitants. A century later, it bypassed the three million mark, as the city described by historian Michael Llewellyn Smith as a "Los Angeles of the Mediterranean" finally spilled onto its own littoral and started climbing the foothills of the mountains that ring the Attica Plain.

Stranger still, while it may have spent a great deal of its history languishing as a backwater of the Ottoman Empire, Athens was already a metropolis with a magnificent past before people were even starting to build huts in what would become the great cities of Europe. So much so, in fact, that many historians talk of Athens as a city already consumed by a nostalgia for its past as it entered the fourth century BCE. Paradoxically, Athens would have to wait until the 1830s for that nostalgic passion to be sated, in an orgy of what the modern city's most eloquent historian, Eleni Bastéa, has called "archaeolatry", worship of the past (although as some Greek intellectuals have bitterly noted, it was an orgy hosted by German occupiers—or what the Athens media of the time sourly dubbed the "Bavarocracy").

While Cádiz lays claim to the title of oldest continuously-inhabited city in Europe, in the Mediterranean Basin only Damascus and Jericho have revealed the remnants of settlements older than those in Athens (and all three are Chalcolithic, or, Bronze Age). Official chronologies date Chania, on Crete, Larnaca, on Cyprus and Thebes, modern-day Thiva (north-west of Athens) as older than post-classical Athens, but none has had the longevity of this pocket-sized "City upon a Hill". Thebes had an important role as a major rival to Athens and Sparta in the region's early history, while Larnaca (the Phoenicians' Kition) remained on the margins of the Greek narrative. Chania, far older than the Cretan capital Heraklion (founded in the seventh century CE), has important links to Crete's history in Mycenaean and "Minoan" cultures, although Arthur Evans' theories about Minoan culture on Crete took a dusting in Cathy Gere's robust dismantling of the Minoan myth in her book *Knossos and the Prophets of Modernism*.

Founding Myths

Across time spans as lengthy as these, even "Greece" itself becomes a nebulous concept: an exonym, a word used by outsiders but never, originally, by those it named, its etymology is usually agreed to have derived either from the people of an ancient town, Graea, in Euboea (modern Evvia), which either traded with or sent migrants to what we now call "Italy", where the new arrivals were blessed with the adjectival Graikos, or possibly from the name of an ancient ruler of the region. Homer called the tribes of Thessaly "Hellenes", a word possibly deriving from regional myth, and Aristotle is believed to have been the first writer to use the words "Greece" or "Greek". The region's earliest inhabitants, proto-Indo-European nomads from Asia Minor, have been lumped under the generic name of Pelasgian, while later groups have to be identified by their individual social and tribal names, such as the Achaeans, Aeolians, Dorians and Ionians. Confusingly, the last of these nowadays lend their name to the islands and people of the Greek archipelago between the foot of Italy and western Greece, but originally they were Greek-speaking inhabitants of what is now Turkey, named after the mythic hero, Ion, who was "invented", according to historian Robin Waterfield, "to be a founding-father of all the Ionic-speaking communities in Asia Minor". The Ionians settled most of the Greek mainland, including that archipelago south of the Adriatic, and became synonymous with the Athenians. What would nowadays be called "identity politics" for these early Greeks is a philologist's conundrum, based variously on era, locality or political affiliation, and one usually accompanied by legions of prefixes and suffixes, but at least this promiscuous border-hopping in early Europe belies any latter day claims to nationalist purity.

No such confusions of nomenclature attend Athens itself: Athina in Greek, Athenai in classical Greek (a plural denoting both place and the later city-state). Its name comes from its protecting deity Athena, in all her competing guises, and whose worship has been dated back to Crete in the fourth century BCE by sources from Plato to Robert Graves. Famously, she sprang from the forehead of Zeus fully-formed and clad in armour, and later competed with Poseidon to become protector of the then-nameless city. She would also, of course, disrupt Poseidon's plans to wreak revenge on the upstart Odysseus at every dramatic turn in *The Odyssey*, and aided Jason in his pursuit of Medusa.

Differing but complementary versions of the myth named her Athena Polias, Pallas Athena, Athena Parthenos and Athena Nike. She was also worshipped under other, lesser epithets in Athens and elsewhere, and was later equated with the Roman goddess, Minerva. As Athena Polias ("of the city"), she was charged with protecting the metropolis that took her name. In the guise of Pallas Athena she was the goddess of civilization, warfare, wisdom and other qualities. Athena Parthenos ("virgin", from the manner of her birth and hence the term for asexual reproduction, parthenogenesis, in addition to the name of her temple, the Parthenon) was inspired by the virginal qualities of the goddess, although the 38-foot statue of her, the one those sailors used to navigate by, was replete with the symbolism of war, not least the figure of Nike, goddess of victory, standing in her hand, and it was in this form that she was deified in her own temple on the Acropolis. The Athena Parthenos statue, a marvel of chryselephantine (gold and ivory), was clad with two thousand pounds of gold (some believe her temple was actually a treasury for the ancient city), which was later melted down to fund the city's military. The statue vanished in mysterious circumstances some time after the fifth century CE, although various replicas remain, including, bizarrely, a modern one in a full-scale simulacrum of the Parthenon in Nashville, Tennessee.

Little is known about Athens prior to the intense programme of building inaugurated by Pericles in the fifth century BCE. Along with Pylos, Thebes and Tyrins, it was one of the major cities in the Mycenaean culture that occupied the central Peloponnese in the years 1600 to 1100 BCE, the twilight of the region's Bronze Age. Nothing remains of Mycenaean Athens apart from the massive foundational Cyclopean walls of a Mycenaean fortress on the Acropolis. Various theories have been proposed to explain the end of Mycenaean Greece, from disasters to warfare with neighbours— notably the Dorians, one of the four main tribes of classical Greece, who occupied Crete, the Peloponnese and other regions. Robin Waterfield argues a subtler thesis that the Dorians "infiltrated" Mycenaean Greece and Athens, and that Mycenaean culture subsided beneath waves of internecine warfare, a recurrent trope in Greek history up to the present day.

In the "Dark Age" that followed the fall of Mycenaean Athens, the city's contours if anything contracted, as large numbers of people either left or fled the city, to other settlements in Attica, other regions and even out to the islands. The next, and most dramatic, stage of the city's development was under Pericles, for reasons personal and political that we will explore later. Developments on the Acropolis had continued after the Dark Age, notably under Peisistratus and Themistocles. The latter reconstructed earlier walls demolished during the Persian destruction of the city in 480 BCE, and built a surrounding wall that "determined the size of the city of Athens for centuries to come" (Waterfield). This irregularly-shaped fortification, with the Acropolis rock at its centre, was barely one and a half miles square and would today be bounded by Syntagma Square and Pireos, Dionysiou Areopagitou, Arditou, and Stadiou Streets.

Pericles went further. As well as instigating the construction of the Parthenon, he also ordered the outlandish Long Walls to be built between Athens and Piraeus, to defend the city's connections to its seaport (although they too would later be destroyed). Nothing remains of the Long Walls, except in conjectured sketches of their route, although some foundations from this era remain, rather abandoned, in the backstreets of Piraeus (near the end of Syntagmos Pezikou). This project, at first augmenting an earlier wall built by Themistocles to defend the route to Faleron harbour, which Pericles abandoned to concentrate on the superior moorage at Piraeus, now provided a fortified corridor running the five miles between the walled city and its port. The Long Walls survived until the end of the Peloponnesian War (431 to 404 BCE), although they also provided a perfect conduit for the plague that killed a third of the population in 430 BCE (Pericles included) as the besieged and enclosed city proved an ideal breeding ground for the disease. The population of Athens at the time is estimated to have been around 100,000, and the devastation of the plague, followed by the defeat of Athens by the Spartans and the Peloponnesian League, was to pave the way for the rule of Philip II of Macedon, his son Alexander the Great and, finally, Rome.

The map of Athens remained more or less static during successive centuries, until the city was sacked by the Roman general Sulla in 85 BCE, when many public and private buildings were destroyed—although others, such as schools, were retained. The peak of Roman Athens came in the second century CE, with the crowning of the noted philhellene Hadrian as emperor in 117. As he had done elsewhere, in Britain and Spain, Hadrian embarked on building projects to glorify himself and his empire, including his Library, still visible in the Monastiraki district today, and the "suburb" of

Hadrianopolis, in the area now covered by the National and Zappeion Gardens. In return, the Athenians built the monumental sixty-foot Arch of Hadrian, also still visible if somewhat marooned on Lisikratous Street, with its famous inscriptions of "This is Athens, the former city of Theseus", on one face, and "This is the city of Hadrian, and not of Theseus" on the other. He also names one of the main thoroughfares of the modern Athenian tourist zone, Adrianou Street, which leads to the Library and the lovely neighbouring Tower of the Winds, another Roman treasure, although precisely who commissioned it remains a mystery. Other Roman benefactors (it is worth noting that the Romans were largely welcomed by the Athenians) also expanded the outline of the city, including Herodus Atticus, who built the vast amphitheatre in the shadow of the Acropolis and completed the Panathenaic Stadium, out beyond Hadrianopolis on the edge of the tiny modern-day suburb of Pagrati. This would provide the ground plan for the first modern Olympic stadium in 1896.

A Long Decline

By the third century, Athens, like Rome, was in decline. The region was poorly defended against attacks from northern invaders, starting with the proto-Goth Heruli, who sacked the city in 267 CE, destroying parts of the Acropolis and the Roman Agora and setting fire to the Parthenon—after which Athens was refortified within the perimeters of the earlier city, leaving the Agora outside the new walls. Again, the contours of Athens shrank, and what remained inside its walls went into steep decline: people fled or were driven from the city, and the land around the Agora began to revert to farmland. In 376 CE the Goths, in fact Visigoths under Alaric, returned and again laid waste to the battered city.

By 529 CE, Athens was under the Byzantine Empire, and the advent of Christianity saw the Erechtheion, Thiseion and Parthenon temples converted into churches—the last dedicated to the Virgin Mary. The city and its environs, however, were almost abandoned during the sixth and seventh centuries. Its people departed to the villages and towns of Attica, its monuments largely in ruins, Athens entered its very own long siesta, and one from which it would only really rouse in the eighteenth century. History did not entirely pass it by, however. It suffered numerous invasions during its centuries at the edge of the Byzantine Empire, under successive waves of Eurasian Avars, Slavs, Burgundians, Franks, Catalans, Florentines and Venetians, most of these on their way somewhere else, and each incursion reduced both the city and its inhabitants. There were periods of Byzantine Athens when the city's fortunes revived, thanks to small-scale industry and trade through Piraeus, and the later Byzantine period, particularly the tenth and eleventh centuries, saw the city expand again—marked by some of the Byzantine churches still standing at some distance from the Acropolis, such as the Old Cathedral on Mitropoleos Street—but the population did not rise above eight thousand at its peak.

Athens similarly languished during the long centuries of Ottoman rule (1485-1833), when its northerly sibling Thessaloniki was the centre of administration. The city shrank back to the perimeter of the Acropolis, its monuments left where they had been knocked down or razed, or, worse, used as materials for Ottoman defences. Structures outside the Ottoman fortifications were abandoned to grassland and haphazard farming. The Acropolis suffered the greatest damage during the Venetian siege on Ottoman Athens in 1687, when a cannonade split the Parthenon roof and ignited a Turkish munitions store inside, shattering a large part of the temple and even sending debris flying over the attackers behind their cannons on the neighbouring Mouseion Hill. At this time the city's population was barely more than seven thousand, and to add insult to injury, when the Venetians did manage to take the city, they abandoned it as strategically useless in less than six months. The Turkish forces dismantled much of the temple of Athena Nike to build defences, and both Turks and Venetians looted the contents of the Acropolis sites.

The New Athens

The details of the War of Independence are addressed in more detail in Chapter 4, but by the time Athens was established as the country's new capital on 18 September 1834, with a new constitution and a new monarch, Otto of Bavaria, installed by the Protecting Powers (England, France and Russia), Athens was finally about to return to the glory of fifth-century BCE Periclean Athens, albeit via Paris, Versailles, Berlin and Karlsruhe, in the paradox that saw the "New Athens" designed chiefly by German architects and town planners swept up in the nineteenth-century craze for neoclassicism.

The first plans for the "New Athens" were produced by two young architects, Stamatios Kleanthes and Eduard Schaubert, the former Greek (he fought in the War of Independence), the latter German, who had studied together in Karlsruhe and Berlin, and arrived in Greece in 1830 with a letter of introduction to Ioannis Kapodistrias, the first governor of the newly established Greek state. Although Kapodistrias was assassinated in 1831, the victim of a feud with a powerful regional clan, Kleanthes and Schaubert were in the right place at the right time, and found themselves "the first civil architects of the new state" (Bastéa). After a few trial projects, Kleanthes and Schaubert were commissioned to produce a design for the new city. Even though Athens had not been named as the new capital—Greece was then administered in Nafplion, seventy miles south-west of Athens at the head of the Argolic Gulf, where the nation's newspapers poured scorn on the idea of Athens as the new capital, while Lord Byron lobbied on behalf of Ioannina, Ali Pasha's city of minarets by its lake in the mountains of Epirus—they approached the project as though it already was the capital. Nafplion was a major business centre, with buildings, services and communications in place to serve the existing administration, whereas Athens, as the media repeatedly pointed out, had none of these facilities. But if a new German king (or to be strictly accurate, the trio of German regents who would represent him until the seventeen-year-old Otto turned twenty, when he could assume the throne) was going to build a new capital for the new country, then by the rules of Romantic philhellenism it had to be built around the site of the Parthenon.

Eleni Bastéa's history of the modern city, *The Creation of Modern Athens*, is tellingly subtitled *Planning the Myth*, and indeed if the New Athens was going to represent the new nation on the world stage, it would require a gargantuan act of self-invention. The myth to be planned was nothing less than fashioning an entire country out of thin air, armed only with the memory of those eight thousand years of history and a few ideas about how other countries conducted themselves. Kleanthes and Schaubert knew that their city would have to compete with Berlin, London and Paris, and if it was going to house a king at its centre, then where else would two ambitious young architects look for inspiration other than André Le Nôtre's plans for Louis XIV's Versailles? Kleanthes and Schaubert's plans underwent numerous revisions, before being unceremoniously dropped for financial reasons, and were extensively reworked by yet another German architect, the noted neoclassicist Leo von Klenze, but you can still discern a faint tracing of Versailles, a trio of boulevards radiating out from a monumental palace, in the street plan of central Athens today.

At the time that Kleanthes and Schaubert were concocting this heady fantasia, however, Athens was still a small town of barely twelve thousand people, mud streets, a shocking absence of infrastructure and a historic centre around the Acropolis which bore all the dents, cracks and bruises that eight thousand years of historical traffic had inflicted. The Acropolis was still a mosque (only one Byzantine church was open and functioning at the time) and there were no restaurants, inns or hotels in the Ottoman town. The British historian and philhellene Christopher Wordsworth described what he saw on a visit in 1832: "The town of Athens is now lying in ruins. The streets are almost deserted: nearly all the houses are without roofs. The churches are reduced to bare walls and heaps of stones and mortar." Worse still, this landscape was about to be transformed into a hot and dusty building site for the next few decades.

In his brief time as governor before he was assassinated, Kapodistrias and his administration had "set the foundations for a national army, an administrative bureaucracy, and an educational system" (Bastéa). His government also established a system to control and promote the modernization of Athens and other cities, using the "modern" concept of grid-like town layouts (in this respect, the renovation of Athens invites interesting comparisons to another bravura project, Ildefons Cerdá's grid-based Eixample extension of Barcelona in the 1850s). Over one hundred and seventy towns across Greece were modernized in this fashion during the nineteenth century. Bastéa quotes one civil engineer, the Corfiot Stamati Bulgari, describing the new grid-shaped towns as symbolizing nothing less than the passage "from barbarity to civilization".

First, though, someone had to shoo the shepherds and farmers off the slopes of the Acropolis.

As visitors to the city's Benaki Museum will discover, Athens' comparative youth places its birth at a fascinating point in recent historiography, when photography began to augment and then supplant paint as a recording tool. As we saw in the comparison with London and Paris in the 1820s, while Athens had expanded, haphazardly, under Ottoman rule (in theory, around modern-day Plaka and Monastiraki, you are walking in Ottoman as well as Roman footsteps), much of Athens was still open countryside. At one point on the Benaki's second floor, photographs start appearing in among the watercolours of Athens, Piraeus and elsewhere (including some by Edward Lear). In 2009 the museum published a selection of images from the collection of art historian Konstantinou Tripou (*Athina: Metamorfoseis tou Astikou Topiou*; "metamorphosis of the urban landscape"), which presents a photographic timeline of the city from around 1850 to 1950. Among other things, it records that in 1855 the temple of Athena Nike was a pile of broken statuary; in 1860 the Parthenon resembled the site of a major earthquake; in 1870 Dionysiou Areopagitou, the street that runs beneath the Acropolis, was still a tree-lined country lane; in 1897 a fence surrounding the Areopagitus rock was being used as a washing line, hung with men's long johns and in 1900 the Theatre of Dionysus still offered vistas of open countryside stretching to the horizon.

Tripou's photographic collection recorded something else, of course: a whirlwind of construction that saw the city explode outwards during the second half of the nineteenth century. As well as the key building projects in the city centre, which are considered in more detail in Chapter 2, Tripou's collection shows that the city's suburban expansion accelerated at a rate probably not seen in any other European city before: by 1910 its suburban railway network (the underground section, only the second such system to be built anywhere in the world, opened in 1896, thirty-two years after the London Underground and eight years before the New York subway) had already reached the opulent villas and mansions of the leafy upper-class enclave of Kifissia, eight miles north of the city centre. Today Kifissia remains the terminus for the northbound Line I of the Attikos Metro.

What Tripou's photographs did not show, however, was the city's rapid expansion in other directions as well, particularly to the southwest and towards Piraeus, along the natural corridor of commerce and dormitory areas following the very first railway line between city and seaport, parallel to the route of the ancient Long Walls. Here, as in other quarters of the city, Athens saw an influx of the rural working class in search of employment.

The expansion of the city was accelerated to a near catastrophic speed in the aftermath of the Asia Minor Disaster of 1922, when an one million Greeks were expelled from Turkey, and about a third of that number of Turks from Greece, following the Turkish victory in the Greco-Turkish War of 1919 to 1922. While many of the displaced went to Thessaloniki, and some to designated islands such as Chios, an estimated 300,000 arrived in Athens and Piraeus, swelling refugee camps below the Acropolis, inventing shanty settlements such as Nea Smyrni ("New Smyrna") out of previously uninhabited countryside and taking over parts of Piraeus. This overnight population boom prepared the ground for the modern conurbation of Athens that stretches from Kifissia to Piraeus today. The displaced who swamped Athens created what historian Mark Mazower has called Greece's "first genuine urban proletariat", and a proletariat, moreover, that would prove a natural breeding ground for working-class resistance during the Second World War and, later, the Civil War of 1946 to 1949. The slum districts of that urban proletariat also produced the most enduring cultural phenomenon of twentieth-century Greece: the "Greek blues" of *rebetiko*.

If Kleanthes and Schaubert's dreamed-of city was already over-subscribed before the first roads were laid, the sudden near-doubling of the city's population from just over 400,000 to more than 700,000 in the space of mere months after the Asia Minor Disaster put an extraordinary strain on Athens. While the plans of Kleanthes, Schaubert and von Klenze still defined the city centre, beyond that Athens stretched into chaotic, and congested, urban sprawl. There were positive side-effects: the influx of workers helped increase industrial development across the country and boosted tax revenues. But the human inundation of an already overcrowded city set the stage for the teeming metropolis of today, which officially topped the four million population mark in 2010, the year that George Papandreou's PASOK government announced an urgent new initiative to promote decentralization of business and population away from the big cities.

While the outline of Athens was not altered by either the Nazi occupation (1941 to 1944) or the Civil War (1946 to 1949) which was already underway before the Second World War ended, both would, along with the Asia Minor Disaster, affect both city and country and their ability to develop after the war. Greece actually prospered after the war, thanks to an estimated five billion dollars provided over succeeding decades through the US Marshall Plan, which bolstered its economy, particularly shipping, agriculture, metals, textiles, chemicals, services and, later, tourism, all of which were headquartered in Athens. Both wars and the later junta of the Colonels (1967 to 1974) are considered in Chapter 4, as are more recent events, only one of which can really be said to have altered the perimeter of the city: the 2004 Olympics. The pros and cons of the Athens Olympics will be argued for years to come, and ultimately it may prove impossible to equate their cost against the prestige they purchased for both capital and nation, but they at least resulted in the transformation of the city's Metro system into one of the finest urban rail networks in the world, and put one of its minor stations, Irini, on the world map. Renovated for the Olympics like many other stations and new extensions, Irini is the stop to get off at to admire the 2004 Olympic stadiums, including the signature white arches of the Spanish architect Santiago Calatrava. In a city that has yet to acquire a true skyscraper, let alone a modernist marvel to rival those in Berlin,

London, Madrid, Paris and elsewhere, Calatrava's Olympic structures are a bold stride into the future, even if, on the evidence of his
work in his home town of Valencia, they might not be around as long
as the Parthenon.

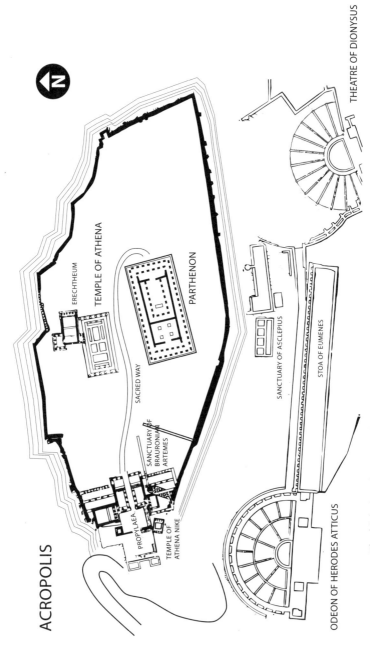

ACROPOLIS

N

ERECHTHEUM

TEMPLE OF ATHENA

PARTHENON

SACRED WAY

SANCTUARY OF BRAURONIAN ARTEMIS

PROPYLAEA

TEMPLE OF ATHENA NIKE

ODEON OF HERODES ATTICUS

SANCTUARY OF ASCLEPIUS

STOA OF EUMENES

THEATRE OF DIONYSUS

The high city: the Acropolis is best approached from Dionysiou Areopagitou, via Akropoli Metro

2 | The Urban Map
Growth and Development

The earliest street plan of Athens is probably a rough sketch, lost long ago, of a path crossing the fifth-century BCE Athenian settlement and culminating in a dramatic stairway leading into the Propylaea, the monumental entrance to the Parthenon, which still greets visitors to the site. This would have been the plan submitted to Pericles for the first stages of major construction on the Acropolis, after the earlier Mycenaean fort on the site and two earlier temples to Athena had been destroyed. Before Pericles initiated his plan, Athens consisted of little more than the Acropolis, various religious and civic structures outside the Acropolis complex, and dormitory settlements huddled around the base of the Acropolis hill. Pericles' plan was to make Athens (and its ruler) the glory of the known world, as would the plans of Hadrian in the second century CE and the architects Kleanthes and Schaubert in the nineteenth. In what we might consider a form of town-planning clairvoyance, both Hadrian and the Kleanthes-Schaubert team, as well as their German and Greek successors, would channel Periclean Athens in their own projects.

The newest street plans of Athens are probably also rough sketches, mostly hidden in the works of post-modern urban theorists or queer psycho-geographers such as Ioannis Vamvakitis, in his snappily titled book *Homosexuality, Identity and Space in Contemporary Athens/Greece: Athenian Queers 'Out for a Walk'*. It is in the spaces between the old and the new Athens that we find the living city, where the next generation of twenty-first century Athenians are finding different ways of mapping their city. These spaces are, by their very nature, off the itineraries of most guided tours of the city, but they also often overlap with the busiest thoroughfares, and in a city where extreme wealth lives cheek by jowl with extreme poverty, they are often less than a city block from each other.

Also between the old and new lies a palimpsest of layered maps of the city through the past two thousand years, most of them also lost long ago, but some, such as the Kleanthes and Schaubert plans for the New Athens, being restored and preserved in the city itself and abroad. This constitutes a vertical mapping of the city, sometimes literally in the case of ancient sites (such as the discovery of Plato's Academy in the 1920s, or the bed of the "lost" Eridanos river in the 1990s) unearthed during construction of new projects. As well as recording its shape through the millennia as its contours expanded, shrank and flexed again, some of these maps also show us how the city was used by the different cultures that occupied it, how some of their plans were adopted and improved on, and how some of them were abandoned or erased. Eleni Bastéa's *The Creation of Modern Athen*s collects many examples of Athens mapped through the ages, including, to give just one example, the partial reconstructions of maps of Ottoman Athens produced by Dimitris N. Karidis at the National Technical University of Athens in 1981. Maps can also be used to tamper with the future: for example, a small but intense academic industry has burgeoned around the decoding of the Enlightenment hero Rhigas Velestinlis' 1797 *Charta*. This Borges-like map of Greece before there was a Greece, which constituted an act of cartographical treason against Ottoman rule that cost Velestinlis his life, is explored in Vangelis Calotychos' *Modern Greece: A Cultural Poetics*. The map itself can be seen in all its hubristic glory at the National Historical Museum on Stadiou Street.

As anyone who has spent any time around maps will tell you, these flat representations of lines, shapes, numbers and words frequently contain more than they seem to, although it is also true that maps are sometimes used to obscure information, or as propaganda, to distort or elide the truth. Sometimes maps, especially Greek ones, are edited, or are simply ineptly produced. Any tourist map of Athens today will show you how to find the Acropolis and many other famous monuments besides, but it may not necessarily tell you where to find this writer's favourite relic, the Tower of the Winds (the southern end of Aioliou Street) or, for that matter, the location of the new Acropolis Museum or the National Museum of Contemporary Art (respectively, Dionysiou Areopagitou and Vasileos Georgiou Streets: both museums are too new for most maps). It will probably fail to tell you where to find the Technopolis arts complex, or the Michael Cacoyannis Foundation performance centre, or Bios, the hipster music-arts hangout (Pireos Street, all three) or the brand new Onassis Cultural Centre (Syngrou Street), either. Even in the era of Google, as checking these last few lines proved, you are sometimes still dozens of tiresome clicks away from this minor but vital information.

Conversely, the same map may often contain information hiding in plain sight, only revealed by cross-referencing with other sources and often offering intimate detail of how earlier Athenians lived and died. Thus a map of Roman Athens will tell you where Hadrian's innovative water aqueduct ran (it drove straight through the heart of wealthy, modern-day Athens, Kolonaki) and where the citizens voted, worshipped, shopped, bathed and went to school. A map of Periclean Athens will tell you where the Long Walls to Piraeus began, and, as we hazarded with the modern coordinates of the wall built by Themistocles, the size of Periclean Athens, and what was protected inside and what abandoned outside when the shape of the city changed. Professor Karidis' reconstructed maps of Ottoman Athens will tell you where the Ottomans worshipped, shopped, bathed and went to school. Similarly, information in the books of historian Mark Mazower will help you identify the place where the Nazis rounded up Athens' Jews (the synagogue on Melidoni Street) or where, startlingly, British aeroplanes strafed units of ELAS, the Greek People's Liberation Army, in a suburb of Athens (probably Pagkrati, above the Panathenaic stadium) during the early days of the Civil War. What Athens really needs, of course, is a Walter Benjamin of *The Arcades Project*, an undertaking far beyond the capabilities of either this book or author, but one that might perhaps have appeared if the writer Nikos Gabriel Pentzikis had been born here instead of Thessaloniki, where his *Mother Thessaloniki* binds the writer's imagination to a multi-layered street map of the city.

The Ancient City

Athens in the fifth century BCE constituted the Acropolis, several structures in and around the ancient Agora ("market"—the commercial and civic meeting place) and perhaps two main streets: the Dromos (Greek for "road") or Panathenaic Way, the route of the climactic procession in the great annual Panathenaic festival, and the Tripod Road, linking the Theatre of Dionysus and the Agora, named for the tripods lining it in celebration of past successes in the theatre (modern Tripodon Street follows at least part of its route). A minor path, the Peripatos, encircled the Acropolis (much as it encircles the etymology of the modern "peripatetic") and provided access to the temples. The *polis*, city, was easily contained between the Thiseion and the theatre of Dionysus. The Thiseion (after Theseus, whose remains it housed), the largest of the structures and still the most dramatic after the Parthenon, was also known as the Hephaisteion, a temple to the god Hephaestus, whose epithet embraced technology, blacksmithing, fire and volcanoes.

In between the Thiseion lay a dozen or so civic structures, notably the Bouleuterion, the meeting place for the city's council, or *boule*; the Strategeion, which served the same function for the *strategoi*, the generals who ruled the city (among them Pericles); and the Tholos, the circular residency of the *prytaneis*, presidents of the boule, elected from their individual communities. These buildings were augmented by a mint, law court, jail and a fountain house where the city sourced most of its domestic water, as well as religious sites such as the *stoa* (porch) of Zeus, and the Altar of the Twelve Gods, where votive offerings were made to the city's tutelary deities: Aphrodite, Apollo, Ares, Artemis, Athena, Demeter, Hephaestus, Hera, Hermes, Hestia, Poseidon and Zeus. Historian Robin Waterfield, who counted the feet and divided by two, estimates that at its fifth-century BCE peak, Athens had a male population approaching forty thousand, a good half of whom would be on standby attachment to the army, either at officer level or as *hoplites*—armed volunteers. In contemporary terms, that is a population comparable to the total of either modern Corfu or Rhodes.

It is worth contemplating that in the fifth century BCE the polis of Athens had a sophisticated political infrastructure that went far beyond what any modern-day Corfiot or Rhodian might ever require: this was an administration for an empire that, at its height, ruled almost every sector of sea that its ships could reach. That sophistication went beyond its politics, architectures and arts (in its first hundred or so years, the Theatre of Dionysus would see the premieres of works by Aeschylus, Aristophanes, Euripides and Sophocles) to inform a subtly graded class system, with a growing middle class. It is interesting to consider that Athens then already had a middle class, while in England the appearance of this division is popularly dated to fourteenth-century references in Chaucer.

Dark Days

Athens would never regain the glory of its Periclean heyday and its decline was swift and ugly, precipitated by imperial hubris, what Robin Waterfield calls "the fifth-century myth: an ingrained belief in the city's right to greatness". Following the defeat of Athens by Sparta at the conclusion of the Peloponnese War in 404 BCE, the Spartans tore down many of Pericles' defences, notably the Long Walls that had defended the city's lifeline to the sea at Piraeus, and as we have seen, the city limits actually shrank. It would take the arrival of the Romans in the second century BCE, and particularly the later rule of Hadrian (76-138 CE), before the city expanded, although Caesar had inaugurated the new Roman Agora in 47 BCE. As well as building the Library and accepting the Athenian tribute of his Arch, Hadrian is also believed to have built temples to Hera and Zeus, a gymnasium and a pantheon, all now lost. Hadrian extended the city with the wealthy suburb of Hadrianopolis: by the time Hadrian arrived in Athens, the city was in a state of disrepair, and Hadrian's New Athens reached as far as today's Benaki Museum. The progressive emperor also poured money into the city's infrastructure, such as the twenty-five-mile underground aqueduct bringing water from Mount Parnitha to a reservoir on the Lycabettus Hill, where the aqueduct and reservoir remained the city's key source of water until falling into disuse in the fifteenth century under Ottoman rule. These innovations came late in the Roman Empire, and within a century Athens, like Rome, was again in decline, and poorly protected against incursions from the north, which came with the first waves of the Goths and Visigoths in the third century CE.

After the depredations of these successive attacks, the period of Byzantine rule had negligible impact on the city, beyond the establishment of numerous churches and, in times of commercial revival, working and dormitory suburbs edging beyond the perimeters of the Roman city: Athens all but vanishes from the history books in this period. Even its most notable historian, Michael Akominatos, Bishop of Athens from 1175 to 1205, described it as a "god-forsaken hole in a far corner of the empire". War drove many people from the city, and the Greek and Roman monuments were either left to collapse into the vegetation that ran riot through the nearly empty city or were cannibalized for building materials.

As we saw in the first chapter, Athens and Greece passed through many centuries of invasion by most of its near and distant European neighbours, the city's fortunes fluctuating depending on the whim of each invading army, but its population never rose above a tenth of that at the height of the rule of Pericles. Even four centuries of Turkish dominion, which might at least have offered stability under the hated Ottoman rule (and we have to acknowledge that some Greeks thrived in the Ottoman economy), saw Athens languish in the shadow of Thessaloniki, the hub of Ottoman Greece.

Towards the end of the Ottoman era, as re-mapped by Dimitris Karidis, Athens had shrunk back to a *chora* (old city) and an *exechoro* (outer city), smaller than the outline of the Themistoclean wall, which had been augmented in 1778 by a Turkish fortification that ran alongside the remnants of the earlier wall. Within the wall the city was divided into eight *mahallas*, or districts, which included Plaka and Psirri, and these were divided into thirty-six *platomata*, "openings", synonymous with parishes. In the early nineteenth century almost all religious, social and civic functions were conducted in or around the Agora. Given the general disrepair of the city, and the disinclination of its rulers to develop it, it seems that the city was only being held for purely strategic purposes.

Athens Reborn

All of which makes the spectacular transformation of Athens in the nineteenth century even more remarkable, as is the constellation of circumstances that brought it about. Held back, or simply abandoned, for thousands of years, Athens took to the modernizing programme with the alacrity and vigour of a young city such as New York or Chicago, or the late twentieth-century "tiger economy" boom towns of Hong Kong and Singapore. Such was its impatience to grow, in fact, that within a matter of decades it was already tripping over itself.

Greece woke up on the morning of 6 February 1832 with a new king and a new constitution that was ratified by the London Protocol of 7 May that year. Athens was to be the new capital of the newly constituted country, but it lacked a single paved road or a single building to house the nation's new administration. Ioannis Kapodistrias, had been made interim Governor of Greece in 1827 under the Protecting Powers of England, France and Russia, who had imposed a truce in the war between Greece and the Ottoman Empire. Despite widespread criticism for his autocratic tendencies, Kapodistrias set about installing an infrastructure for the nascent state, including new structures for its government, army, education and urbanization systems, which in 1832 were still headquartered in Nafplion. Kapodistrias in fact employed Kleanthes and Schaubert, who had arrived offering their services for free, and began work with decidedly modest educational projects, before Kapodistrias offered them salaried employment. It was in the chaos of the interregnum between Kapodistrias' assassination in 1831 and Otto's coming of age in 1834 that Kleanthes and Schaubert were commissioned to design a whole new city.

While some of their plans were abandoned due to cost factors and were altered by architect/painter Leo von Klenze (commissioned by Otto's father, Ludwig of Bavaria), Kleanthes and Schauberts' vision, like the faint ghost of André Le Nôtre's designs for Versailles, can still be discerned in a street map of Athens today. Some buildings, such as the royal palace, were shifted across the city in von Klenze's refit, as were some of its offices (the parliament, originally housed in a grand neoclassical building on Stadiou Street, nowadays the National Historical Museum, later moved into the palace, although only after the monarchy had decamped). Even though Kleanthes and Schaubert began drawing their city before it was even confirmed as the new capital, they clearly knew that the smart bet was on Athens, and set about "planning the myth", as Eleni Bastéa describes it, accordingly.

The heart of the new city was Otto's Square (today's Omonia), which was the original choice of site for the new palace, with the three radial boulevards of Pireos, Athinas and Stadiou each meeting Ermou as it crossed the centre of the city between the old, Acropolis municipality and the newer city. Otto's Square was the apex of an acute triangle with Ermou as its base and Pireos and Stadiou as its sides (Stadiou, like Pireos, is one of the city's oldest thoroughfares, probably dating back to the construction of the Themistoclean wall). With the southern flank of the Acropolis marked out by Dionysiou Areopagitou Street, this network constituted the new city centre. Stadiou was soon joined by two equally grand boulevards parallel to it, Akadimias and Voulevariou, later renamed Panepistimiou ("university"), where most of the new city's neoclassical monuments were to be sited.

Otto's planned palace was moved twice, from Kleanthes and Schauberts' preferred location of Otto's Square (where it would have been linked directly to the Acropolis by Aioliou Street) to von Klenze's choice of a position near the Thiseion, before it was finally built at the Boubounistra Gate, an ancient entrance on the Themistoclean perimeter now lost beneath modern-day Syntagma Square. This decision was another intervention by Ludwig, who was lending Greece the money to build the palace. Originally the "front garden" of the palace, Syntagma ("constitution") acquired its name and its status as a public square when Otto declared a constitution from the balcony of the palace in 1843 following the popular uprising against the monarchy and government known as the 3 September 1843 Revolution. The palace's leafy "back garden", planned by Otto's queen, Amalia, and said to have been one of the most ambitious planting projects in Europe at that time, was also later turned over to the people and renamed the National Gardens.

The establishment of the National Gardens laid a new eastern border to the city limits: the new Irodou Attikou Street at the bottom of King Otto's "garden", running up to meet Vassilissis Sofias at the corner where the Harokopos family mansion later became the Benaki Museum, was outside the city boundary. Its most imposing mansion, the Presidential Palace, designed by architect Ernst Ziller, is nowadays the official residency of the prime minister. When it was completed in 1897, the palace looked east across open fields. Today, according to a 2008 report in *Kathimerini*, Irodou Attikou is the most exclusive strip of real estate in Greece, with prices starting at €25,000 per square metre.

This sketched the shape of the central Athens that we know and walk today. From this core, its map outline resembling, perhaps a little fancifully, a deep-draughted yacht sailing east, possibly towing the Acropolis rock back towards Mount Hymettus, the city quickly developed armatures such as Vassilissis Sofias, where the fantastically wealthy burghers of nineteenth-century Athens built equally fantastical mansions, such as those that now house the Benaki and Cycladic Art Museums.

This touches on another subject that Eleni Bastéa considers at length: just who bankrolled the Kleanthes-Schaubert-von Klenze plan for the New Athens? But we should first consider other features of the new city. As the newspapers of the time were beginning to comment, having lost their campaign to keep the capital in Nafplion, Athens was suddenly turned into a vast building site, and one that would be busy well into the twentieth century and beyond. Yet a photograph in Bastéa's *The Creation of Modern Athens* suggests that even as late as 1880 the south side of Syntagma (that is, opposite the Hotel Grande Bretagne) opened on to woodlands, and photographs from the Benaki Museum's Konstantinou Tripou collection attest to the presence of woodland on that side of the square as late as 1905. In 1870, Dionysiou Areopagitou Street, beneath the Acropolis, was flanked on the other side by fields of crops. The same year, the Thiseion was photographed surrounded by nothing more than fields of prickly pear. Also photographed the same year, Patission Street, heading north from the Archaeological Museum (opened in 1889), looked like a lost highway from the American Mid-West, or perhaps Siberia. Yet within a decade all of this would be transformed into one of the smartest cities in Europe, albeit one still a little rough around the edges.

As well as competing with London and Paris, this "New Athens" also had to represent the new Greece to itself, to foreigners and to the swelling Greek diaspora overseas. In this respect, it was something rather more than Cerdá's Eixample extension in Barcelona: no mere dormitory suburb, the New Athens was tasked with reinventing the cradle of civilization and giving it a capital city worthy of the name. Stamatios Kleanthes later described the ambition to create a city that would be "equal with the ancient fame and glory of the city and worthy of the century in which we live".

Their original plans were to eradicate the "old" city—the Greek, Roman, Byzantine and Ottoman centre—and replace it with modernist grids and long, wide boulevards, while retaining as much as possible of the archaeological detail around the Acropolis. These plans would prove both too costly and too radical for the neoclassicist who re-drew their plans, Leo von Klenze, which is why the tangled warrens of Plaka, Monastiraki and Psirri look like they do today. Eleni Bastéa seems to read a colonial attitude, of a space as a *tabula rasa* on which outsiders could raise a city almost theme-park-like in its perfection, in the approach of not just Kleanthes and Schaubert, nor of von Klenze either, but of the German diplomats and administrators and the Greek politicians who attended its birth as well.

Beyond the confines of the old city and in between the satellite settlements outside it, the Attica Plain was little more than sporadically farmed badlands, with the thin long line of Patission Street heading north. If it was an opportunity for the city planners to impose their will on an untamed landscape, it was also the place where they would have to construct the shop front, back office and living quarters for the new king and his new country. In Athens and elsewhere, Bastéa writes, "New buildings and towns came to be considered among the most inalienable proofs of progress and national accomplishment. In fact, architecture and town planning were in many cases the only proofs of progress."

Both criticisms and critics of the New Athens were legion. Public, media and politicians were divided over both the intent and the physical plans for the new city, although few projects on a scale such as this pass without criticism. But some were unavoidable, such as the comment by the newspaper *Athena* in July 1835 that "to tell the truth, the seat of the Greek state does not at all differ from an African or a Turkish city." A French visitor three years later described Athens as "a town which does not yet have a road, but where they started building a palace," although as Bastéa points out, both St. Petersburg and Washington DC boasted similar grand structures before they had pavements outside them. In 1858, when the building project was well underway and plans for the new Academy on Panepistimiou were announced, the newspaper *Aion* laughed: "We have no ships, no army, no roads, but soon we will have an Academy. Turkey, beware!"

This would at least seem to confirm Eleni Bastéa's comment that the construction of the New Athens was as much about public image, and how the new state was perceived abroad, as it was about laying roads and drains and building palaces and academies. For the politicians, she says, "Europeanization, connection with the ancient past and cleansing of the immediate Ottoman past were the government's stated goals." "The newly-planned cities," she adds, "adorned with neoclassical civic structures, were seen as tangible symbols of progress towards 'enlightened' Europe, of internal political and cultural unity, and of the break from the Ottoman rule." This itself, however, proved divisive: the "progress" towards modernity, and a northern European modernity at that, was at odds with the conservatives who saw tradition and the reclamation of the former capital in Constantinople as the true path for Greece. This dream of an alternative Greek future was unlikely to survive in a set of circumstances where Greece's future had been delivered into the hands of northern Europeans. Politically, financially and aesthetically, the new Greece's future lay in Europe, not Asia.

Modern Capital

The expansion of Athens was aided by the largesse of wealthy Greeks living abroad, as self-made multi-millionaires purchased immortality in return for underwriting monuments such as the National Library and the Academy, and chipping in seed money for projects such as the National Archaeological Museum as well. Private money also underpinned charitable projects including schools, orphanages, hospitals, even a prison. Where the rich, expatriate or domestic, really excelled themselves, however, was in their own palatial bricolage. The proliferation of mansions along the tentacular avenues also served to highlight a growing imbalance between the haves and have-nots. The expansion of the city's wealthy zones, thanks largely to the growth of trade, agriculture, metals and shipping in particular, was in stark contrast to the city's lack of public schools, electricity and sewerage, to the extent that the poorer parts became the breeding grounds for disease and, a theme that continues to play in certain districts in the twenty-first century, social unrest.

By 1900, Athens had a population estimated at 125,000—already three times the expected occupancy in the Kleanthes-Schaubert-von Klenze plans, and it showed in the sprawl that was beginning to eat its way into the surrounding countryside. It had been transformed, Bastéa writes, "into an elegant capital with a number of new buildings: a palace, a parliament, and a new cathedral, as well as a university, an academy, a national library, a refurbished ancient stadium, newly-built private residences and several tree-lined squares and boulevards." Those squares and boulevards were lit by gas and, later, electricity, and trains and trams rumbled along the streets as well as beneath them. A 1911 map of the city shows it beginning to edge into Exarheia, Kolonaki and north just beyond the Archaeological Museum. By 1922 the centre had spread to embrace most of the inner suburbs, although Ambelokipi and Kipseli were still beyond the city limits. A map from a decade later, 1932, shows Kipseli and Ambelokipi still outside the city, although with dormitory areas sprouting outside both and creeping up Patission Street as far as Ano Patission station—but most remarkable is that Piraeus had, in the space of a decade, expanded to almost the same size as its parent.

The reason for this was a dramatic rise in the city's population, recorded in official census reports for the years 1921 and 1922, from 413,000 to 718,000, a near-doubling of the population that might be considered a conservative estimate given the reliability of census figures in a country like Greece at that time. The cause of this sudden influx was one of the most shameful humanitarian disasters of the twentieth century, variously known as the Asia Minor Catastrophe, the Great Fire of Smyrna, the Smyrna Massacre or even the Greek Holocaust, in which as many as a quarter of a million Turkish Greeks and Armenians died, directly or indirectly, at the hands of Mustafa Kemal's troops following the Turkish victory in the 1919-22 Greco-Turkish War. We will consider the political events in more detail later, but the immediate effect of the Turkish victory was the violent expulsion of a million Turkish Greeks, some to the islands, some to Thessaloniki, but at least 300,000 to Piraeus and Athens, where the already over-populated city found itself unable to cope with the new arrivals. Shanty towns and canvas refugee camps sprang up, such as Nea Smyrni outside Athens and Kokkinia in Piraeus. The pressure on the infrastructure of the city was so great that a US engineering company was hired to renovate Hadrian's aqueduct and reservoir, which had been partly destroyed by the retreating Turks in 1832, and construct a new supply system for both Athens and Piraeus.

The largest of these new settlements was Kallithea, an ancient settlement designated a city in 1884, partly as a centre for events in the 1896 Olympics (it also hosted events in the 2004 games) but also as a depot for the Athens-Faliro railway line in 1910. Today it is the fourth largest municipality in metropolitan Athens, the eighth largest in Greece and the second most densely populated area in Greece after Neapolis in Thessaloniki. The "city" of Kallithea stretches from just beyond the Filopappou Hill to the former sea resort of Faliro. It saw the biggest influx of refugees after the Smyrna Disaster, although it had also seen arrivals from the eastern Mediterranean and Black Sea region during the "Greek Genocide" in the Ottoman Empire of 1914-23, in particular some of the estimated 180,000 Greeks expelled from the Pontus region on the southern shores of the Black Sea who would continue to arrive following later waves of ethnic repression in Pontus. With their own language, Pontic, which diverged from the main linguistic stem of Greek in pre-Christian times, and their own culture—their music would become a root for *rebetiko* in Athens and in Thessaloniki—they were and remain one of the most distinctive of the native ethnic groups in Athens.

With Kallithea, and other refugee zones such as the aforementioned Nea Smyrna, Kokkinia and Nea Ionia and Kaisariani, we can see a geographical drift by the poor and the rich of Athens from the 1920s onwards. While the poor naturally congregated in the south, west and east of the centre, near the port and the commercial corridor between port and city (although they were priced out of the smarter sections of the coast), the rich migrated to leafier areas in the north or the swanky parts of the "Athenian Riviera" around Glyfada, nowadays vaunted as the "Hellenic Hamptons" (its more likely unofficial twin would be Marbella), and its younger rival of the 1960s, Voula.

It was doubly unfortunate for Athens, and the nation as a whole, that these waves of refugees arrived when Greece was virtually bankrupted by the cost of the Greco-Turkish War. Athens was barely able to build a fraction of the housing needed, and had to rely on the Red Cross and the League of Nations for material support for the refugees. Yet despite the global impact of the 1929 Depression, Greece actually saw an increase in productivity in the 1930s, thanks in part to the availability of cheap labour in the slums of Athens and Thessaloniki. This too would be short-lived, brought to a brutal halt by the German occupation of Greece in 1941. Considered in more detail later, the German occupation demolished the Greek economy, although it did put it in place for regeneration with help from the post-war Marshall Plan following the traumas of the Second World War and the Civil War. Athens saw a boom in urbanization in the 1950s and 1960s, in which the Los Angelization of the city through road construction and the serried ranks of white mid-rise apartment and office blocks went along with the destruction of much of the city's older infrastructure.

The 1950s also saw one last, curious and short-lived change in the mapping of the city. An undated map from the early 1950s records Stadiou and Panepistimiou as, respectively, Roosevelt Avenue and Churchill Street, both renamed after the Second World War by a grateful Greek government but, it would seem, largely ignored by an ungrateful Greek public, whose insistence on referring to them by their older names saw the street names revert shortly afterwards.

By the 1960s the street plan of Athens was being drawn on the hoof by three forces: politics (governments of both left and right were responsible for crimes against urban planning aesthetics), economics and demographics. The trick for politicians of any shade was to accommodate an exploding population within the city's geographical limitations and budgets that were at best parsimonious. Even the Colonels—the military junta that ruled from 1967 to 1974—found themselves throwing up brutalist high rises and surrendering more and more of the city to the motor car. As arterial roads and the cross-hatched dormitory areas between them marched out towards the mountains and the sea, the city developed its very own Los Angeleno smog problem, colloquially known as the *nefos*, a highly acidic mix of carburettor exhaust and industrial emissions which in one report was estimated to have killed two thousand people in 1975 alone. In 1982, when acid rain from the smog was starting to eat the monuments on the Acropolis, the city introduced its first attempts at traffic control. It took until the 1980s, when Athens experimented with Mexico City-like restrictions limiting car access on alternate days depending on licence numbers (and inspiring a similarly Mexico City-like boom in duplicate licence plates) and later traffic-calming measures combined with plans for the Metro system and other transport innovations, for the nefos problem to subside. Today, with an estimated ratio of one car per two people in the metropolitan Athens area, there are still two million people driving around the city dreaming of a parking place.

It would also take the 1990s, and the approach of the 2004 Olympics, for the cash-strapped city to start addressing the state of its streets. Having suffered the embarrassment of losing its bid for the 1996 Centennial Olympics—celebrating the hundredth year since the first modern Olympics were staged in Athens—due to International Olympic Committee concerns over traffic and pollution, the city was stung into action to prepare for 2004. It embarked on a plan almost as radical as Kleanthes and Schaubert's to remodel the city from the centre out, starting with pedestrianization around the Acropolis. The pedestrianization continues to spread, with Athinas Street the next likely candidate, but it would take an extraordinary transformation of collective will for Athens to become a pedestrian-friendly city.

For the time being, the streets of the city centre remain a nightmare for the elderly, infirm and anyone whose mobility involves a pram or wheelchair. But those shortcomings noted, Athens would not be Athens without the lively spectacle of its streets and pavements, and the communities that resist (or simply, in their decay, defy) gentrification even in the heart of the inner city. Exarheia, alone, is an island of the alternative culture that vanished from cities such as San Francisco, New York, London and Amsterdam decades ago. There are suggestions, however, not least in neighbourhood action groups across Athens, that a growing number of PWAs (pedestrians with attitude) are planning to wrest back their city from the internal combustion engine.

3 Landmarks
Buildings and Styles

The icon that has represented Athens for over two thousand years—the Parthenon atop its peripatetic outcrop of limestone, the Acropolis hill—comes wrapped, sometimes literally, in complications. It has spent more of those two thousand years down, in various stages of disassembly, than up, and when it was up it was as often as not masked as something else: fort, mosque, harem, Christian church. It has been largely or partly destroyed at least four times, by Persians, Spartans, Venetians and Ottomans, and in 2009 filmmaker Panos Koutras sent the whole Acropolis up in flames—but we will get to that later. Early attackers, such as the Persians, set fire to or razed parts to either show their dominance or destroy symbols of a theology they did not follow. Later attackers looted the site for its valuables, or simply took some of the best bits home with them. During periods of occupation, the Parthenon's stones were used to build newer structures, many also later lost or destroyed. Throughout its thousands of years of abandonment, it was also used by the Athenians themselves as a handy nearby supply of free building materials.

Even when the Parthenon fell into the hands of sympathetic custodians—which we can date to August 1834, when Leo von Klenze officially initiated the restoration of the site—it would still be (and still is) some way off resembling the original structure. As the historian Mary Beard has pointed out, it spent most of those millennia in the service of cultures other than the one that built it, and it is only from our modern northern European perspective that the "first" Parthenon is considered the important one (many modern Greeks, while revering the original, might side with Professor Anthony Kaldellis, author of *Hellenism in Byzantium*, in cleaving closer to the Byzantine version). We can never revisit Pericles'

Bomb site: The worst damage to the Parthenon was the 1687 cannon attack by the Venetians

Parthenon, only fashion reconstructions such as the one in Nashville. Even beyond contemplating what it might be like if the Elgin Marbles were returned (they would go to the nearby Acropolis Museum, anyway), or reminding ourselves that we must imagine how it looked with the statuary painted and interiors decorated, there is a far more prosaic fact to be considered: throughout the modern period, and throughout the history of photography, the Parthenon has hardly ever been seen, or photographed, without a section obscured by scaffolding or cladding, or without that iconic profile punctured by cranes. That essential signifier of all things Greek—the clump of Doric columns held together by the *crepidoma* at the base and the pediments at the top—has been fashioned into a million and one things, from souvenir snowstorms to whimsically shaped ouzo bottles, and reproduced on surfaces ranging from tea towels to a recent Athens Gay Pride t-shirt, but only in an idealized, almost cartoon-like fashion, and never with the metal and wooden prosthetics that have wrapped it ever since von Klenze ordered the lamps to be lit across the Acropolis and Athens itself on 28 August 1834 to launch the renovation.

Of course, we have to come to an accommodation with representations of any historical monument: we are contentedly ignorant about the original appearance of Stonehenge, for example, and are still half a century away from seeing Gaudí's Sagrada Familia as he intended and without two hundred years' worth of scaffolds and cranes. And representational authenticity can only go so far: did we really need that Venus de Milo with the arms that a thoughtful forger kindly added, or, indeed, Arthur Evans' steel-reinforced concrete reconstructions at Knossos? We appear to be at ease with our archetypal Greek sign as it was recorded when Edward Lear last passed by with his watercolours and brushes in his knapsack, even though Edward Lear was probably the last person who saw it like that.

The Meaning of the Parthenon

The infamous Thomas Bruce, the seventh Lord Elgin (1766-1841), who arrived in Athens to sketch the Parthenon and left with a significant collection of its assets, was by no means the only vandal to have embarked on a shoplifting spree among the Parthenon columns: sizeable pieces had vanished from the site before his visit in 1801 and continued to vanish after his workmen left in 1812. Some of those pieces are still in museums from Copenhagen to Rome, via the Louvre and the Vatican. Elgin's crime, it seems, was in the sheer amount of ancient treasures he removed, estimated to represent half of the artefacts at the site, and his claim that he had permission to remove material, in the form of a *firman*, or permit, from the Ottoman sultan, has never been satisfactorily proven (his defence, when he was called before the British parliamentary committee which exonerated him, was to produce an Italian translation of the firman written from an aide's memory; the original has never been found). As authorities such as Mary Beard have also pointed out, the Parthenon artefacts were in a terrible state of disrepair by the time Elgin arrived anyway, and the Ottomans considered them as little more than debris. Even so, Robin Waterfield pointedly observes that Greeks defending Athens from the Ottomans were so desperate to save their heritage that they offered the Ottomans Greek bullets to deter them from taking lead from the Parthenon structures to make their own ammunition.

The argument over the ownership of the Parthenon Marbles, as it seems only polite to call them, has become mired in what is little more than a high-brow curatorial dispute. The Greeks have now built a hyper-modern museum where the Marbles could be reunited with the pieces that Elgin could not carry off, which seems to leave the British shouting, as one British Museum director did, about "cultural fascism" when countering the arguments for the return of the Marbles. In the summer of 2010, the British Museum's Parthenon exhibit came fifth (that is, last) in an online list of must-see highlights at the museum, below the Rosetta Stone, exhibits from Ancient Egypt and Babylon, and even below a promotional campaign with online games designed to appeal to pre-teens who would, in any case, find mobile reception terrible if they visited the place itself. Even here, the Parthenon seemed to feature mainly in the museum's gift shop, where you can buy a replica of the Horse of Selene for £995, VAT included. In considering the feelings of those who might be robbed of the opportunity to experience the partial Parthenon Marbles out of their original context at the British Museum, a cynic is tempted to ask how many people within reasonable travelling distance know where it is, how to get there, and what they would see if they did. There is also the uncomfortable fact that the era of budget air travel has made Athens quicker and cheaper to get to than London for any Briton living north of, say, Leicester.

The Parthenon functions at other levels as well, of course: at the heart of those Doric columns is the elegant mystery of the Golden Ratio (or Mean, or Section), the almost mystical mathematical ratio of 1:1.68—*pi*, or *phi*. The Golden Ratio can be found in nature from the proportions of crystals to the nautilus shell to the shape of dolphins to the human body (Leonardo da Vinci's famous diagram of a naked man, for example), and from the rings of Saturn to a little-known quirk in Heisenberg's Uncertainty Principle only discovered by quantum physicists in 2010. The apparent presence of the Golden Ratio in the proportions of the Parthenon is even more of a.mystery in a structure long thought to have been improvised as it was going up, and more than a hundred years before Euclid began to explore the uncanny recurrences of pi in the natural world.

Beyond the humorous ouzo bottles and Gay Pride leisurewear, the Parthenon also symbolizes a profound sense of national identity, although given the long and complicated history of both building and nation that symbolism has to be considered in terms of polysemy, or multiple interpretation: what one Greek reads Pericles' clump of Doric columns to mean probably varies from what another Greek reads it to mean, and the possible variations of meaning are almost infinite. Like most national symbols, however, its purview is generous, even though that may leave it open to misappropriation. Its importance as a national symbol explains the touching anecdote about the Greek soldiers offering their own bullets to the Turkish enemy in the hope of saving the Parthenon, and also the popular urban myth from the Second World War that tells of a young Evzone, the elite army squad that nowadays guards the Parliament, who wrapped himself in the Greek flag and hurled himself to his death from the Acropolis rather than lower the flag on the orders of the Nazis.

This Zelig-like character from recent Greek history, who was given a name, Konstantinos Koukidis, and even a photographic portrait in the myth (the photograph can be found on the net, but curiously the Koukidis trail goes cold there) did not in fact exist. An expert on Evzone history at the National War Museum, Yannis Mylonas, told the weekly English-language *Athens News* in April 2010 that the story is a "myth", adding, "This person does not exist." Koukidis was probably invented by the right-wing wartime government in order to counter the real-life legend of young left-wing activists Manolis Glezos and Apostolos Santas, who famously tore down the Swastika flag from the Acropolis at the start of the occupation and were hailed as heroes. (Glezos, in his early twenties at the time, went on to become an admired politician, author and environmental engineer, and is still active in his late eighties: he was tear-gassed in the face during a demonstration in Athens in 2010, the pictures making the front pages of the press and the evening TV news.) The Koukidis myth, believed to originate in wartime propaganda written by a Cypriot journalist, continues to recycle itself in weird little internet versions of those Greek roadside shrines, helped no doubt by a plaque still in place on the Acropolis slopes hymning the imaginary hero, despite the fact that archive newsreel footage exists of the Nazis quite tidily removing the flag themselves.

The competing Glezos/Koukidis mythologies, one true, one not, the latter invented to spite the former, and itself a measure of the conflict between patriotism and party politics during the war, are perfect examples of that polysemy surrounding the Parthenon-qua-Acropolis and its fundamental role in national identity. In their 2009 graphic novel *Logicomix*, a number one on the *New York Times* Best Sellers List, authors Apostolos Doxiadis and Christos H. Papadimitriou have a character (in fact, a walk-on part for Papadimitriou) say, "Henry Miller said that *true* Athenians never come near the Acropolis." Doxiadis and Papadimitrious' droll conceit is probably a joke within a joke, and one that we will also be considering later, but it also refers to the contradictory attitudes that natives sometime have towards their domestic monuments: do New Yorkers visit the Statue of Liberty? Londoners their Tower? Parisians their Tour Eiffel? (Well, Barthes and de Maupassant did, although both only to escape the view of it from everywhere else in Paris. Similarly, try avoiding the view of the Acropolis on a stroll through downtown Athens. You can't.)

It is possible that what Doxiadis and Papadimitriou are saying is that Miller's "'true'" Athenians would not be seen dead visiting something that has been turned into a tourist attraction—Robin Waterfield comments that: "The well-meaning restoration of the Acropolis in the first quarter of the twentieth century… [focussed] on creating a tourist attraction rather than on historical reality"— although it is more likely that they are having a joke at the expense of Henry Miller and his breathless love letter to Greece, and to Athenians in particular, *The Colossus of Maroussi*.

Perhaps what they are also implying is that Athens needs newer icons. We could consider contemporary architect Manolis Anastasakis' outrageous whorled "'multiskyscraper'", West Athens Towers, intended to represent three curled olive leaves pointing sky-wards, but at a planned 660 feet in height, some way—approximately 572 feet, in fact—above current Athenian planning restrictions, still just a glint in the eye of one of Greece's most innovative architects. Anastasakis' breathtaking design, envisioned for a site some distance from either the Acropolis or the neoclassical monuments of the city centre, is just one of a number of avant-garde projects proposed for Athens since the 1985 General Building Code was enforced, which first reduced the permitted height of new-build projects to 105 feet and, later, down to eighty-eight. While aimed chiefly at standardiz-ing building practice in an earthquake zone, the code effectively robbed Athens of a skyline for which many Greek modernists yearn, and which might have alleviated the pressure on the spread of a hor-izontal city notorious as a sprawl of indifferent and often plain ugly low-rise developments thrown up on the cheap. (Its tallest building so far, the 337-foot, twenty-eight floor Athens Tower, built in 1971, has survived several six-on-the-Richter-and-above earthquakes un-scathed, while smaller buildings fell down.)

The Athens Trilogy

With little sign of any imminent change in Greek or Athenian planning laws, we are left to consider those monuments built before the
1985 Code. Chief among these, both aesthetically and chronologi-
cally, is the "Athens Trilogy"—the Academy, National Library and
University, handy neighbours on Panepistimiou Street—and the
trilogy is almost as interesting for the politics behind its construction
as for its architectural splendour.

The Academy, the one that *Aion* newspaper thought would scare
the Turks, is the grandest of the three, not least in its echoes of the
Acropolis' Erechtheion in the exterior façade, and the statues of
Athena and Apollo guarding the entrance from the tops of two imposing Ionic columns. Many people, among them at least one newspaper editor, did not think that the new city had any urgent need for
an academy in 1885. The expatriate Greek millionaire Baron Simon
Sinas, then living in Vienna, had told the Greek government that he
would like to donate a building to the new state, and an ambassador
came up with the idea of an academy. The job went to the Austrian
architect Theophil Hansen, whose student Ernst Ziller completed
the project, as he did Hansen's designs for the National Library.
Hansen had designed Vienna's Hohe Haus, or Parliament building,
which the Academy in part resembles, but he was also already responsible for the National Observatory on the Nymfon Hill (1842)
and would oversee the later Zappeion Hall (1888). Sinas, who was
also a diplomat in addition to being one of the wealthiest men of his
time, funded many philanthropic projects in Austria and Hungary as
well as Greece, and also poured money into Hansen's Observatory
(in a roundabout form of thanks, Sinas now names a crater on the
Moon, some eight miles wide and one-and-a-half deep, in the Sea
of Tranquillity), but according to Eleni Bastéa his riches ran out
before the Academy was completed and the Greek state had to underwrite its completion.

The National Library, begun in 1887 and finally completed in
1902, had a similarly complicated birth. King Otto had called for a
national library as early as 1858, and in 1885 the three Vallianos
brothers, Greek millionaires living in Russia, led by Panayis Vallianos

(he stands on the plinth outside the Library and was known as the "father of Greek shipping", the industry from which he made his fortune), donated a million drachmas to build the library. Theophil Hansen again got the job, and again his student Ziller completed the project. An idea of the value of the Vallianos donation to the library might be gauged from a 2003 Bank of Greece study which noted that in 1832 the Great Powers loaned Greece sixty million drachmas to underwrite the recovery of the country and the development of new industries. At a sixtieth of the Great Powers loan, the Vallianos donation was funding one very fancy library.

The cornerstone for the new University was laid in 1839 (the University had been founded in 1837, when it was temporarily housed in the home of Stamatios Kleanthes) but did not open its doors to students until 1841. This time the commission went to Theophil Hansen's brother, Christian, and if you are beginning to wonder if this might have seemed a little incestuous, well, the Greek press was wondering about that as well. Complaints about the "Bavarocracy" and their friends were by now common (although Christian Hansen had been in Greece since at least 1833, and worked on the renovation of the Temple of Athena Nike on the Acropolis) and it was widely believed that Greek talent, which would prove itself with later, if more modest, projects in the city, was being overlooked in favour of superstar architects from Berlin and elsewhere, even when the Greeks tendered below the fees demanded by the Germans. Eleni Bastéa also notes that many of these buildings were conceived as vanity or signature architectural projects, where form outweighed function, and where the form took a very Romantic north European view of how the New Athens should function.

This curious interplay between wealthy expatriate Greeks and German architecture continued beyond the trilogy on Panepistimiou. Leo von Klenze had included a proposal for an archaeological museum in his plans for the city, and in 1856 yet another overseas Greek shipping magnate, Demetrios Vernardakis, living in St. Petersburg, donated two hundred thousand drachmas to begin the project. The committee overseeing the competition for proposals was headed by Ludwig Lange, the Munich Academy luminary who designed the fairytale Dom (cathedral) of Worms and the fantastical Leipzig Bildermuseum. Responses to the call for proposals for the museum were deemed below par, so Lange designed it himself, eschewing the wedding-cake effects of his German projects for the austere neoclassical columns that still greet the visitor to the National Archaeological Museum on Patission Street.

We might date the decline of the Bavarocracy in the construction of Athens' architectural face to the "new" cathedral on Mitropoleos Street, the Evangelismos tis Theotokou (Annunciation of the Virgin), on Mitropoleos (Cathedral) Street, started in 1842 and completed in 1862. King Otto joined Simon Sinas in contributing to this project, with Theophil Hansen again at the draughtsman's board. Hansen's proposals, mixing Romanesque and Gothic styles, were not to many people's liking, and the project was temporarily shelved when funding ran out. In 1846 Otto announced a new competition for a "Byzantizing" design for the cathedral, a tall order as competing architects were expected to invent this new school out of nothing beyond the example of Hagia Sophia in Constantinople. For the first time in a major competition, a Greek architect, Demetrios Zezos, won the commission, signing the first Greek-designed building on the New Athens skyline, although one itself bound up in contemporary re-readings of ancient ecclesiastical architecture.

Zezos died before the cathedral was completed, and the French architect François Boulanger completed the project. When the interim home of the new Greek parliament (which met in a mansion owned by wealthy businessman Alexandros Kontostavlos) burned down in 1854, Boulanger was commissioned to build a new parliament on Stadiou, where today it houses the National Historical Museum. While the likes of Hansen and Ziller were still working in the city—Hansen completed the Zappeion, commissioned by another wealthy expatriate, Evangelis Zappas, who also underwrote the first modern Olympics in 1896, while Ziller designed probably the last great German neoclassical building in Athens, the National Theatre, opened in 1901—the success of architects such as Zezos and Boulanger seems to have broken the spell woven by the Bavarocracy.

The boom times that had enriched the men who bankrolled neoclassical Athens were coming to an end by the close of the nineteenth century. While investment flowed into the country in the 1860s and 1870s, Greece, like the rest of Europe and the USA, was badly affected by the "Long Recession" of the 1870s to the 1890s— to the extent that in 1893 the admired modernizing prime minister Harilaos Trikoupis was forced to make his famous declaration to parliament: "Regretfully, we are bankrupt." This was followed by the almost year-long Greco-Turkish War of 1897, after which a defeated Greece was forced to pay reparations to Turkey and the mediating Great Powers placed the Greek economy under the control of an International Financial Control Commission. Greece also became mired in the First Balkan War of 1912-13, and the Greco-Turkish War of 1919-22, culminating in the burning of Smyrna and the population "exchange" that followed.

The economy improved in the 1910s, to the extent that Athens even enjoyed its own Belle Époque, and the evidence of its art nouveau period can be seen in the Acropole Hotel and Livieratos Mansion on Patission Street and the Ionian Bank on Panepistimiou, as well as the restored arcades running between Panepistimiou and Stadiou, and numerous examples of art nouveau decoration in the streets around Omonia. Surprisingly, perhaps because it is surrounded by 1960s modernist developments, the most notable example of Athenian art deco is the Monument to the Unknown Soldier, below the parliament building on Syntagma. There are at least ten fine deco sites in the city (see the excellent Discover Contemporary Architecture website at http://www.culture2000.tee.gr), but most visitors do not notice the grandest of them all, the former Rex Cinema on Akadimias Street, towards the Omonia end, where seven storeys of pure deco lines soar above the bustle of the busy street.

The DCA website also explores a wealth of twentieth-century architecture around Athens, from the old Hellenikon International Airport, one of the last projects of arch-modernist Eero Saarinen, and Walter Gropius' late-Bauhaus design for the US Embassy, through a plethora of post-Frank Lloyd Wright private villas in the suburbs, and into the era of post-modernism, most visible at the Alpha Credit Bank building on Stadiou and the SATO building on Kifissias Avenue in Maroussi, which resembles a spacecraft en route to dock at The Mall Athens. Most of this architecture was either private or corporate, with the exception of a few mild-mannered modernist projects built for state agencies.

Omonia Square

One single space at the centre of Athens describes the city's journey from the neoclassical late nineteenth century to the post-modern twenty-first, and that space is, perhaps unsurprisingly, Omonia Square. On its journey, it also provides clues to the forces at work changing the face of the city: chiefly, it would seem, the internal combustion engine and, more recently, dramatic alterations in Athens' demography.

Omonia in the late nineteenth century was a circular island of lush, sub-tropical vegetation: palms, bush cacti, pollarded deciduous trees. A wide road and elegant four-storey domestic and retail buildings surrounded it, still below the sightline of the Acropolis half a mile away. By 1905 it had acquired a central bandstand and tall pines appeared among the maturing standard trees. Within a decade much of this greenery had been swept away, metal telephone poles and electric lamps towered above the remaining plant life, and a network of power lines was strung across the square for the trams that now traversed it. By the 1930s the vegetation had disappeared entirely, uprooted during the construction of the subterranean railway station below. In its place, seven art deco columns camouflaging air vents from the station ringed the now oval central space, each column with a statue of one of the seven muses on its square base. The columns, and their attendant muses, fell from favour and by the 1940s only their bases remained as open vents from the underground station. By then the square was already going downhill: the surrounding buildings had undergone changes of use, acquired new frontages and bristled with electric rooftop signs, and motorcars were beginning to outnumber the pedestrians in the street. Blank modernist office and retail buildings appeared on the square in 1950, and the trams were on their way out, replaced by petrol-powered buses and cars.

Omonia had been wholly surrendered to the internal combustion engine by 1960, following the installation in 1957 of a four-lane roundabout. Access to the underground station was shifted to entrances on the pavements around the square, much as it is today, and the centre was levelled and replaced with a large fountain, but one whose grass verges and dominant water feature seemed designed to deter any public access, should pedestrians have managed to get through the traffic. Those elegant late nineteenth-century low-rises had been replaced with blockish, modernist buildings reaching as high as ten storeys. The former "Concord Square" built for King Otto was now a pretty traffic island with any human activities shifted to the pavements, although occasionally it would still be swamped by political rallies and crowds celebrating sporting events. A comparable development in London would have involved running the lower part of Oxford Street across a flattened Piccadilly Circus and carving up Leicester Square to connect it directly to the Strand.

Omonia continued to decline through the 1970s, when large hotels started appearing to serve growing tourism in the city, but, paradoxically, when the area had at the same time been deserted by the middle classes and their culture (homes, shops, cultural centres) and was already attracting comparison with Times Square in New York. Indeed, in a further, ignominious, paradox, the two buildings that would most clearly mark Omonia's decline were hotels, the Bagkeion and Megas Alexandros, designed by Ernst Ziller in the 1880s and abandoned to urban decay by the 1960s (although there is talk of renovating both). As in any urban centre left to its own devices—and we could invoke former no-go zones such as London's Piccadilly, Paris' Pigalle/Gare du Nord and Berlin's Bahnhof Zoo station—it became a focal point for the city's homeless and a also the go-to one-stop for drugs and the unlicensed sex trade (prostitution is legal in Greece, but an estimated ninety per cent of sex workers ply the streets beyond the licensed brothels). It also provided rich pickings for petty criminals preying on hapless tourists trying to get back to those same hotels from the Metro station or nearby tourist sites. Cheap flop houses in surrounding streets became homes for the poor or unlicensed brothels (try negotiating the southern end of Sokratous Street late at night any day of the week), and the square and its side streets became both day space and dormitory for those with nowhere to sleep.

Several half-hearted attempts were made to rehabilitate Omonia in the 1980s, but the area's problems are more social than architectural, and require subtler solutions than either post-modern urban theory or the kill-the-homeless hysterics of media and paranoid tourists. In 1988 it acquired Costas Varotsos' 26-foot neo-Futurist sculpture *Dromeas* (Runner), a clever shattered-glass-and-iron approximation of a blurred image of a running man, but he was withdrawn when in 1994 when Omonia was designated an urban renovation area in preparation for both the rebuilding of the Omonia Metro station and also a new pedestrianization scheme for the 2004 Olympics. (A newer *Dromeas*, taller by thirteen feet, was later planted on a grass verge opposite the Athens Hilton, on Vassilissis Sofias Avenue.)

In 1998 the Unification of Archaeological Sites of Athens project, launched in the 1980s by the Ministry of Culture and Tourism, held a competition for the reshaping of Omonia. A group of young architects from the 1993 class in the architecture school of the National Technical University of Athens—named DKT after its founders Grigoris Desylas, Marialena Katsika and Theodoros Tsiatas—won the competition. Omonia was among the first four projects by DKT, and at that time the group had only seen one other project, a pedestrian bridge across a railway line in northern Athens, completed. Given some of the peachy archaeological sites that were up for grabs during the pre-Olympics renovation of the city centre, bidding for the widely-loathed Omonia was always going to be a poisoned chalice for whoever won first prize. The DKT proposal was bold, if drastically minimal, and deliberately went against traditional notions of what a public space should be, although it returned the centre of the square to pedestrian use and eliminated most traffic from two sides. Unfortunately, without any social function at its centre, it just became an even wider open space for the street people who lived on and around Omonia. Press and public reaction to the implemented DKT design was swift, and harsh: the new Omonia was judged, by even its kindest critics, as a great theoretical idea that had landed on the wrong site.

Shortly after the new Omonia controversy, urban theorist Michail Galanakis (possibly a former compatriot of the DKT team at the same university), published a paper for the European Union's UrbEUROPE research foundation, addressing the issue of Albanian and Eastern European "transnationals", as even the foreign-language expatriate press now calls them, in and around Omonia. In particular, he applied a concept adopted from earlier researches by the Greek architect and fellow urban theorist Dimitris Philippides, who, as Professor of Architecture at the National Technical University of Athens, may well have taught both Galanakis and the DKT team. Galanakis describes Omonia as a perfect working example of what Philippides called "para-urbanism". Para-urbanism, says Galanakis, is "a branch of urban planning that functions side by side [with] official urban planning." It is not something that urban planners sit down and draw with a Rotring pen, but rather "mediates between the state and the citizens", or more specifically it creates "grey" or ambiguous zones where the transnational has to draw the map and negotiate the terrain by her- or himself, without assistance, or sanction, from the state. It allows the state to wash its hands of an unwelcome underclass, while retaining the sanction penalty of expulsion, and permits the underclass to exist precariously in the grey zone.

In an earlier crisis involving a different type of "transnational", Athens responded by building vast tent cities (one around the Thiseion, in the shadow of our friendly Greek signifier, the Acropolis) and new towns that later became the city's suburbs. Those transnationals were, of course, nominally Greek, although Greeks who had elected to live as nominal Turks in Turkey. Today, an estimated 56 per cent of the transnationals around Omonia are believed to be Albanians, and Albania is only a short hop, skip and jump either from Ioannina in Epirus or from the Greek haplotype group to the Albanian one in the human genome map of the International

HapMap Project. Moreover, in 2010 Albania was embraced by the Schengen Area, allowing its citizens free passage across EU borders. We will consider the issues of immigration and race in Athens in a later chapter, but for the meantime, at the end of nearly a century and a half of Omonia's transition from the neoclassical New Athens to the post-modern, post-Olympic city, these liminal citizens of the ultimate liminal zone of Athens are as much a part of the face of the city as the power shoppers of Kolonaki and the Kodak-snapping tourists of Plaka and Monastiraki. The cradle of civilization has yet to find a civilized way to deal with their presence.

4 | Rulers and Ruled
A Brief Social and Political History

> "The ancient Greeks invented democracy, but their linguistic descendants in modern times had to import representative government, a modern version of a democratic polity, from the West. Contrary to what the average Greek believes, this has not been an indigenous product, and its roots do not go back to ancient times: the intervening ages and empires swept away all traces of the ancient democracy."
>
> John S. Koliopoulos & Thanos M. Veremis,
> *Greece, The Modern Sequel*

Given the reputations of the authors—Koliopoulos is Professor of Modern Greek History at Thessaloniki University, Veremis Professor of Political History at the University of Athens—we are unlikely to find a more astute analysis of the cliché that Athens was not only the "birthplace of democracy" but has also somehow been appointed guardian of the concept ever since. As they point out in their dismantling of numerous myths about recent Greek history, events were usually more complex than most histories allow, and the motives of the key players were often ambiguous, if not actually criminal.

Yet even though the democracy adage is a cliché compromised by qualifiers, it is still a cliché worth entertaining. Its etymology (from the classical Greek for people, *demos*, and power, *kratos*) is also a cliché, perhaps better described by one writer as "rule by us". Koliopoulos and Veremis' "ancient democracy" was usually partial and frequently flawed; their reading of the modern version might make you wonder why the Greek voter even bothers to get out of bed on polling day (beyond the fact that voting is compulsory in Greece—hence the madness on public transport around elections, when everyone must return to their birthplace to vote—although so far the authorities have not attempted to prosecute the abstainers).

The politician and poet Solon (630-560 BCE) introduced the earliest form of democracy in Athens, in legislation passed to allow classes below the aristocracy to participate at *some* levels of government. Still, some lower classes were excluded—as were women of any caste, who would have to wait another two thousand four hundred years after the death of Solon until they got the vote—and entitlement in ancient democracy still depended on gender, class and wealth. That privilege was also founded on a profound social inequality: even through the Periclean heyday and beyond, Athens was a society that relied on slavery.

Tyrants and Factions

Solon's experiment was short-lived: considering his reforms done, he left Athens to travel, having extracted a promise that the Athenians would keep his changes in place for at least ten years. They lasted just four before Athens descended into factionalism, only brought to an end by a coup delivered by Peisistratus (c. 580-527 BCE), who staged his own attempted assassination and used the bodyguards detailed to protect him to take the Acropolis and declare himself tyrant, which in those days merely meant an unelected leader. Despite his autocratic rule, Peisistratus was popular, instituted the Panathenaic Games and promoted the arts. Aristotle judged him "the most inclined toward democracy" of the factions in Athens.

Peisistratus was succeeded as tyrant by his sons, Hippias and then Hipparchus. Both outdid their father's ruthlessness and disinclination towards collective government, and both were targeted in a famous assassination attempt by the "Tyrannicides", Harmodius and Aristogeiton, two nobles who bungled an attempt to kill the two brothers and rid Athens of their despotic clan. The Tyrannicides did kill Hipparchus, but Harmodius was killed by the tyrant's guards, and Hippias survived to torture Aristogeiton to death. The Tyrannicides were lionized in verse and statuary as "liberators" of Athens and probably set the stage for the brothers' liberal successor, Cleisthenes (c. 570-508 BCE).

It was in direct reaction to the factionalism during the tyrannies of Peisistratus and his sons that Cleisthenes introduced a dramatic restructuring of power, away from the earlier system based on four dynastic families to ten groups defined by their locality, or *deme*, a system that would underpin much later social organization. More importantly, he introduced a system in which positions of authority were assigned by a lottery vote, rather than by kinship or primogeniture. He is also popularly credited with inventing ostracism, banishment by popular vote: having vanished from public records rather abruptly near the end of his life and career, he is believed by some to have suffered ostracism himself.

The ascendance of Themistocles (c. 524-459 BCE) pushed Athenian democracy still further. He came from an undistinguished background (said by some to be a broken home in an immigrant quarter of Athens) but breached the Athens elite and became *archon*, ruler, in 490 BCE. Themistocles built his famous wall and expanded Athens' navy, moving its port from Faleron to Piraeus and outwitting the Persians at the battles of Marathon and Salamis. Marathon was one of those moment-in-history battles, famously described as "more important than the battle of Hastings" by John Stuart Mill, in which the turn of events might have reshaped the history of Europe.

Pericles (c. 495-429 BCE), hymned by Plutarch and Thucydides, succeeded Cleisthenes and ushered in the Golden Age of Athens, his achievements measured by the fact that the Golden Age is also commonly known as the Age of Pericles. As well as initiating the building projects visible today, he also enacted laws that emancipated almost all Athenian classes above its slaves. As part of his project to glorify Athens, and himself, Pericles transformed the city into a cultural centre. Alas, among his more noted accomplishments was propelling Athens into the Peloponnesian War against Sparta, a political misjudgment nowadays read as fatal hubris. Pericles died in the early years of the war, from the plague that had probably travelled to the city from Piraeus along the Long Walls and incubated in the siege conditions inside Themistocles' wall.

The Spartan victory at the end of the Peloponnesian War abruptly erased the concept of democracy in Athens. Whatever new systems of rule and whatever remarkable civilizations arose or arrived—and they did, with Philip of Macedon, his son, Alexander the Great, and later under Hadrian—rule-by-us was replaced with rule-by-them. The luxury of self-determination was set aside in favour of pragmatism in times of war and invasion, and sometimes the Athenians welcomed the intercession of external forces. Although the Romans razed much of its civic architecture, the city prospered, as it would (when not harried by northern invaders) during the Byzantine period, when power shifted to Constantinople and Athens settled into its long siesta as a backwater.

The demographic profile of the ruled fluctuated, as some occupiers, notably the Romans, imported families and workers. In periods of decline, when much of the population had been driven out by invaders such as the Slavs, the pacified city would be re-populated by settlers from other towns, and from further north, especially the region now marked on the map as Albania. There were also periods, particularly in the Byzantine era, when entire populations were moved from region to region, largely as a means of establishing an ethnic presence in a contested area, such as Thessaly in the northeast. Attica itself remained a largely static agrarian society, and would continue as such until the twentieth century, when emigration to the cities and abroad was, and remains, common.

Towards Independence

As we have already seen, Athens was a distant and inconsequential satellite of the Byzantine Empire—so much so, Robin Waterfield writes, that one medieval historian had to write to Constantinople to confirm that the city still existed. It fared little better in political terms through four hundred years of Ottoman rule, although population growth, shifts in trade patterns and events in northern Europe, particularly in France, began to give some Greeks ideas of their own.

The appearance of the Filiki Eteria ("Society of Friends") in the early nineteenth century, with its heroic motto of "Freedom or Death", has ascended into Greek mythology, as its founders fully intended. The Society took its model from the Freemasons, and was also linked to the Italian underground organization the Carbonari. Its arcane initiation rituals and cloak-and-dagger activities were partly security measures against detection, but also partly theatre. The organization was formed in Odessa in 1814 by three expatriate Greeks, Nikolaos Skoufas, Emmanouil Xanthos and Panagiotis Anagnostopoulos. Skoufas was connected with members of the Carbonari, Xanthos was a member of a Freemasonic lodge on Lefkada, and Agnostopoulos had been a member of an earlier underground liberation group, the Ellenoglosso Xenodocheio, or "Greek-Speaking Hotel". They moved their group to Constantinople in 1818 and began approaching likely co-conspirators. Ioannis Kapodistrias, the future first prime minister and patron of Kleanthes and Schaubert, rebuffed them and later accused the Society of contributing to the chaos in post-revolutionary Greece. They did, however, manage to recruit Theodoros Kolokotronis and Alexandros Ypsilantis, two of the key military figures in the revolution, and the Orthodox Metropolitan (or bishop) of Patras, Germanos, who would be iconized in Theodoros Vryzakis' famous painting, *The Bishop of Old Patras Germanos Blesses the Flag of Revolution* (1865). The blessing of the flag took place on 25 March 1821, considered to be the start of the revolution, and the date has become the nation's greatest non-religious annual celebration, with massed military parades and fearsome airforce flybys in Athens and elsewhere, even though most historians now believe that the event did not, in fact, happen quite like that but is probably a convenient myth conflated from separate occurrences over a period of time.

The Society's main contacts were among the chiefs of the various clans in Epirus and the Peloponnese, who would prove to be power-brokers in the birth of the new nation. They soon took the Peloponnese, and by late April 1821 had besieged the Turkish garrison in Athens. Athens and the Acropolis were taken and re-taken by both sides, with massacres and other atrocities ascribed to each, and the Turks finally surrendered the Acropolis in June 1827. Fighting continued elsewhere, with the Protecting Powers of Britain, France and Russia biding their time on the sidelines before they stepped in and sent their navies to defeat the Ottomans in the Battle of Navarino in October 1827. In 1828 Ioannis Kapodistrias was elected governor of the new state at Nafplion, and found himself with a new country and a new capital to invent—and an eight-thousand-year-old ancient civilization to reinvent.

It is at about this time that the Filiki Eteria, their mountain rebel associates and the military and political figures of the age begin appearing on the radar screen more than capably staffed by Messrs Koliopoulos and Veremis. The Filiki Eteria (whose flag still flutters, quaintly, in back gardens, on balconies and outside restaurants in parts of Greece) and individuals such as Kolokotronis and Ypsilantis became symbolic figures in a romanticized fantasy of what the War of Independence was about. What it achieved is still open to debate. Universal suffrage, which by definition has to include that part of the population born female, only appeared in Greece in 1952, and there was the junta of the Colonels to be lived through before a largely peaceful parliamentary democracy settled on the country in the 1970s.

The Eteria's two main sources of support in Greece were the *klephts* (a Greek colloquialism for thief or brigand), rebels who had retreated to the mountains rather than bend to Ottoman rule and who now waged low-level war against the Ottoman administration, and the powerful networks of rural landowners, who ruled their areas along feudal lines. Neither group was gripped by a vision of a Soviet-style people's republic, but both saw the war against the Ottomans as a perfect opportunity to claw power in their own direction.

Koliopoulos and Veremis have mined deep veins of autobiographical whimsy penned by key figures in the romance, in which they elaborated airily about just how power would be structured when the Turks were swept into the Aegean. These authors concurred that the ordinary Greek was not ready or educated for, or indeed needful of, an "ancient" Athenian democracy. Rather, power would be retained by those who knew better than the great unwashed did. They frequently referred to the need for a "king" or "lord", and in their Homeric yearnings seemed to be waiting for the return of an Odysseus to set his house and lands in order. This latterday wanderer, however, would have to come from their ranks (Ypsilantis, handily already a son of the Romanian aristocracy, was a favourite), and share their narrow, mercantile definition of what a "revolution" was about.

It was against this backdrop of heavily-armed antics in Epirus and beyond that geopolitics delivered victory into the hands of the Greeks at Navarino and Ioannis Kapodistrias into a palace on Nafplion's very own Syntagma Square with the word κυβερνήτης (*kivernitis*), or governor, on the door to his new office. Most accounts of the early days of the new Greek government, from both Greek and English-speaking historians, describe it as chaos, but this was after all a new country and a new society being invented out of fresh air. Kapodistrias was one of the most famous victims of this chaos: his assassination in 1821 was an act of revenge by a powerful clan, the Mavromichalis family, after Kapodistrias had heavy-handedly imprisoned the family head over a political dispute.

The political situation became even more complex in the years following Kapodistrias' assassination, as the Turks held on to other parts of Greece, and the hastily-convened parliament for the new nation proved both premature and ineffectual. It was hamstrung by interference by foreigners—the Protecting Powers were ever keen to foreground their business interests in the Mediterranean and a new Germany monarchy was parachuted in because, as some Greek observers noted bitterly, the Protecting Powers did not think that the average Greek was ready or educated for, nor needful of, a true democracy, either. Matters became further blurred when the new nation found itself in direct physical conflict with the brigands, the landlords or their compatriots, and blurred further still when some of these were absorbed into the hierarchy of the new administration. Many of those involved in the revolution seemed perfectly happy for the previous system to continue as it had done under the Turks—but minus, of course, any actual Turks. The Eteria's proud cry of "Freedom or Death" was beginning to ring a little hollow.

An uneasy compromise between all parties—insurgents, landowners, military figures, politicians, Protecting Powers, Church—was eventually reached that would incorporate aspects of western democracy with indigenous systems of social structure (those klephts sliding into jobs behind big desks in Athens). By the time Otto was old enough to assume the throne, he sat down as king of an absolute monarchy, one whose interests were somewhat at odds with the Eteria's heroic slogan or, at least, how the average unprepared and uneducated Greek might parse the phrase.

Imperfect Democracy

As its circumstances might suggest, Otto's reign was not a happy one, and the twenty-something king may well have been the puppet of his regents and certain overseas parties ensconced behind the arras. While city and state set about refashioning themselves, discontent percolated both in the streets and in parliament, where politicians complained about heavy-handed German rule that sometimes even required them to conduct their business in German. Moreover, Greece was taxed more heavily on a sixty million-drachma loan from the Protecting Powers than it had been under the Turks. Wishful conspiracy rumours circulated, and, in September 1843, coalesced into an actual uprising, popularly led by the armed forces and aided in part by the inmates of the notorious Medrese prison, who mysteriously found their cell doors open the night that the rebels marched on the king's front garden. Otto placated the trespassers on his lawn by promising them a constitution, and the constitution of the new Greece was passed in March 1844, transforming absolute monarchy into constitutional monarchy, in which power would be shared between throne and parliament.

While Otto looked out as the city rose around his new palace on the renamed Syntagma Square and the citizenry muttered on the streets below, Greece's near-democracy stumbled along. As Koliopoulos and Veremis declare bluntly: "the parliamentary records of this period present a dismal picture of parliamentary life." Otto, beset by factionalism among the Greeks, the state's financial problems and disagreements with both Church and parliament, was unseated during an army coup in 1862, when the parliamentary Assembly deposed him, but not before a student attempted to assassinate Queen Amalia and, although foiled, was declared a folk hero in some quarters. Otto was succeeded by King George I (1863-1913), the first of six kings from the House of Schleswig-Holstein-Sonderburg-Glücksburg, and his successors ruled through various political systems until the monarchy was abolished in 1974.

Despite this grim diagnosis, there were still signs of life in the patient. George's fifty-year reign produced two of the finest prime ministers Greece has seen: the admired modernizer Harilaos Trikoupis (1832-96) and some decades later Eleftherios Venizelos (1864-1936), a man some now consider to be the greatest modern Greek ever, while many contemporaries considered him to be the perfect personification of the devil himself.

Trikoupis' eventful career offers a timeline of the problems that Greek democracy faced during his era: between 1875 and 1895 he served as prime minister no fewer than seven times as governments came and went in quick succession. He made his political name with a manifesto published by the Athenian daily *Kairoi* in 1874, entitled "Who's to Blame?", on the monarchy's role in the Greek constitution, and parlayed it into a successful demand that the monarchy ask the winning party in an election to form a government, rather than choosing the one that most suited the monarchy. Trikoupis also implemented other constitutional changes, one of which saw him ousted by his own innovation (he was soon back), and he is credited with instigating plans for a progressive infrastructure of roads, railways and harbours (as well as the Corinth Canal) to give Greece the communications system it needed to modernize its economy. On his last watch he inherited an accumulated national debt that led to his famous declaration to parliament, "regretfully, we are bankrupt", and despite remaining in office for a further two years he failed to resolve Greece's debt problems: he resigned in 1895, spared the humiliation of his party's defeat at a general election months later.

The saintly demon Venizelos was both the product and later orchestrator of a very different set of circumstances (he has also been sufficiently rehabilitated to have had the shiny new Athens international airport named after him when it opened in 2001). His forty-year career spanned the beginning of the Cretan rebellion against Turkish rule in the 1890s and the Greco-Turkish War of 1919-22. In between, Venizelos' name became paired with both the *Megali Idea*—the "Big Idea" of a united Greece encompassing all the Greek-speaking lands lost in the East—and its polar opposite, the National

Schism between Venizelos and King Constantine I over whether Greece should enter the First World War (the pro-German king favoured neutrality; Venizelos saw advantages in siding with the Allies).

The devilish associations were made mainly by his enemies on the Greek Right and those who believed that his pursuit of the Megali Idea had led Greece into a war with Turkey that it was unlikely to win. Venizelos was actually voted out of office (along with his Liberal Party) two years before the burning of Smyrna in 1922, but the events that led to the atrocity had been set in motion much earlier. We have touched on Smyrna before, but it is worth considering further, as it would be one of the three defining events for Greece in the twentieth century. Conservative estimates suggest that a quarter of a million Greeks, Armenians and others were either killed or "disappeared" on forced marches in the events during and leading up to the Turkish massacres and burnings at Smyrna. This was the inspiration for Winston Churchill's ironic contribution to the annals of chaos theory in his famous remark, "it was a monkey bite that caused the death of those 250,000 people"—a reference to the unfortunate death from sepsis of King Alexander after being bitten by a monkey in October 1920. His sudden death, and the defeat of Venizelos' Liberal Party a month later, created a power vacuum into which the right-wing United Opposition party and its hero, King Constantine (who had been forced into abdicating by the Protecting Powers, mindful of his pro-German politics), stepped quite nimbly. With a plebiscite in which ninety-nine per cent of voters called for Constantine to return from exile, the new government set about replacing the appointees of Venizelos' forces with its own, inexperienced officials, and so king and army led the country into the disastrous last two years of the Greco-Turkish War. The catastrophic end of the war saw the king forced into a second humiliating abdication and Venizelos recalled from self-imposed exile in Paris to lead the country again.

The election of December 1923 also saw the Greek government declare a republic, with the consequence that the monarchy was (temporarily) abolished and Constantine's successor, King George

II, was forced to abdicate. Apart from the year-long dictatorship of Theodoros Pangalos in 1925-6, which ended with the ruler being deposed by his own officers, Venizelos and the Liberal Party returned to power a further three times. The election also saw a dramatic increase in the number of parties across the political spectrum contesting the election; from just two in 1922 to more than ten in 1923. The 1926 election witnessed the first appearance of candidates fielded by the Greek Communist Party, or KKE (Kommounistiko Komma Elladas), which had been formed in 1918. The KKE spent parts of the twentieth century underground, but since the fall of the Colonels in 1974 it has usually managed to come a respectable third in most national elections, even into the subsequent era of George Papandreou's PASOK (Panellinio Sosialistiko Kinima). In the twenty-first century, when communism is considered an outdated anomaly even in those countries it dominated for much of the twentieth, the KKE's brand of communism still has a hold on a sizeable part of the Greek vote, even if it rarely wins a fifth of the votes won by PASOK.

Venizelos initiated a still-remarkable reconciliation with Turkey, to the displeasure of many Greeks for whom the memory of Smyrna was still raw, and in 1929 his party swung to the Right with the "idionymon" (special illegal act) law, which effectively criminalized members of the KKE and anyone active in the trade union movement. His Liberal Party was defeated by the People's Party (Laikon Komma) in 1933, which saw the monarchy re-established and King George II welcomed back from exile. Venizelos did his reputation no favours by rashly backing a failed coup against the People's Party in the spring of 1935, which laid the ground for the return of that party in June of that year. The success of the Liberal Party the following January was shortlived, after the "4th of August Regime" in which prime minister General Ioannis Metaxas (in fact, an interim appointment by King George II, who feared left-wing insurrection) used the pretext of a threatened general strike led by the KKE to declare a state of emergency and imposed martial law. Historian Richard Clogg has written that the Metaxas regime was more "paternalist-authoritarian" than fascist, although it is clear that Metaxas was an admirer of both the Italian Fascists and German Nazis, and borrowed ideas from each.

Occupation and Civil War

We have Metaxas to thank for the other major public holiday in the Greek calendar, "Ohi Day" on 28 October, when Metaxas supposedly said no (*ohi*) to the invading Italians at the start of Greece's involvement in the Second World War. It is fascinating to consider how far alliances had shifted during this period for Metaxas to now find himself on the receiving end of an ultimatum from his former Italian friends to either surrender or be invaded. Metaxas is believed to have in fact said "Alors, c'est la guerre" ("so it's war") to an ambassador who delivered the ultimatum from Mussolini at 4am on 28 October 1940. By 5.30am Italian troops were entering Greece from Albania.

The Greek experience of occupation by the Nazis between 1941 and 1944 (the Italians were swiftly, and in cases such as the German massacre of Italian troops on Kefallonia, ruthlessly supplanted) would have a profound effect both on people and nation. This was no mere occupation but the systematic wrecking of an entire country. The Nazis diverted both Greek industry and agriculture to their war effort, commandeering mines and banks, going so far as to shoot individual farmers for concealing their harvests. Hundreds of thousands are believed to have died a result of the famines of 1941 and 1942, some dropping dead of hunger on the streets. According to the Jewish Museum of Greece, tucked into Nikis Street just off the bottom of Syntagma, as many as ninety-seven per cent of the 100,000-strong Greek Jewish population were exterminated or imprisoned domestically and then transported, via a chillingly efficient ticketing system, through the rail networks of southern Europe to the concentration camps in the north. The historian Mark Mazower, in his finely-researched *Inside Hitler's Greece*, believes that the Nazi depredations on Greece had the unintended effect of strengthening the resolve of the Greek resistance, not least in propelling Manolis Glezos and Apostolos Santas up the flagpole on the Acropolis to tear down the Swastika flag.

The nation and economy exited the Second World War in a disastrous condition, but it is interesting, and not a little disconcerting, to note how some of the big guns were being realigned even before the war ended for Greece. The Greek Left had worked with the Allies throughout the conflict, but its ambitions for post-war Greek democracy became an increasing worry to the Allies as the end of the war approached. Here, however, contrasting interpretations of events can lead to some ambivalence. Koliopoulos and Veremis are unequivocal in considering the KKE a serious threat to Greek democracy in the run-up to the civil war of 1946-9, whereas Mark Mazower believes that the KKE, abandoned by Stalin in a gentlemen's agreement to carve up post-war Europe among the superpowers, was more a threat to Churchill's desire to thwart communist expansionism. Mazower in fact goes as far as to say that the KKE-led ELAS (Ethnikos Laikos Apeleftherotikos Stratos, or National People's Liberation Army), decided *not* to attempt a takeover of the country. Nevertheless, as early as 1943 British officials were having discreet meetings with Nazi counterparts about the supposed communist threat to "British strategy in the Eastern Mediterranean". Two months after British troops liberated Athens, on 12 October 1944, those same troops were fighting Greeks on the streets of Athens. This better-dead-than-red policy led to British aeroplanes strafing outposts of the EAM (Ethniko Apeleftheropo Metopo, or National Liberation Front) and ELAS in what today are the smarter areas of middle-class Athens.

Mark Mazower is, however, unsparing in recording how the Left's early, lofty, ideals—healthcare, education, women's suffrage—descended into self-destructive factionalism. For the general population, the civil war was if anything worse than occupation, pitting Greek against Greek and locking Greek politics into a Left-Right binarism that persists today.

Left and Right

Two coalitions, on the Left and Right, were the main contenders in the first election after the war in 1946, with the Right, led by the People's Party, emerging clear winners with three times the votes gained by the Left. It was notable, however, for the appearance on the national stage of George Papandreou, father of Andreas and, in 1952, a no-doubt proud grandparent to the current occupant of the Presidential Mansion. Papandreou had been a close aide of Venizelos, served in various posts in governments under Venizelos and others, and his newly formed Democratic Socialist Party crept up on the Liberal Party vote before forming a short-lived alliance with it in 1952, with Venizelos' son Sophoklis at that point leading the Liberals.

The Greek Right held on to the government until 1963 when Papandreou, by now head of the new Centre Union party, defeated Constantine Karamanlis in the wake of the continuing scandal over vote-rigging in the 1961 "Violence and Fraud" election of Karamanlis' National Radical Union. The Karamanlis government was already in serious trouble following the assassination in May 1963 of the popular United Democratic Left leader Grigoris Lambrakis, whose brutal killing in public was the inspiration for Vassilis Vassilikos' best-selling novel Z, later turned into a classic of modern European cinema by Costa-Gavras. Over half a million people attended Lambrakis' funeral, which swiftly turned into a demonstration against the government. Vassilikos took his title from the graffito "Z" (from the Greek, Zoi, or life, with the Z here standing for Zei, "he lives") which began to appear on walls across Greece following the death of Lambrakis.

Enter the Colonels

Papandreou's Centre Union won the following election in 1964, but lasted only a year before politics began to dissolve into the chaos that culminated in the appearance of tanks on the streets of Athens on 21 April 1967 announcing the coup by the Colonels. The Colonels' rule was in fact a series of different regimes, including one failed attempt by King Constantine II to stage a coup within the coup. The leader of the Colonels was Georgios Papadopoulos, himself unseated in an interior coup towards the end of the regime in 1974, and instigator of a gruesome campaign of terror against anyone considered an enemy of the state. One of the many ironies of the junta was that its two chief ideologues, author Georgios Georgalas and journalist Savvas Konstantopoulos, were both former Marxists.

In an earlier, more malleable, age, the military regime might have passed for just another swing to the Right in Greek politics, comparable to the regimes of Papagos and Metaxas, but it was actually a product of its era, launched against the perceived threat of changes that were happening around the world. As well as the expected clampdowns on left-wing activists, trade unionists, media and anyone who might be labelled liberal, youth culture in almost any form was considered anathema. Yet Greece actually experienced an economic surge during the Colonels' era thanks to investment by the likes of Coca-Cola, and perhaps the most unlikely paradox is the fact that the military presided over the birth of mass tourism in Greece, even if young male visitors found themselves undergoing an unexpected haircut at Athens airport if their hair was deemed too long.

Papadopoulos himself was unseated in an internal coup in 1973, after his plans to "liberalize" the regime were denounced by his hardline successor, Dimitrios Ioannidis. Ioannidis authorized the attempted military coup in Cyprus by EOKA-B, the right-wing nationalist group formed out of the original EOKA, which opposed British rule on the island. The Ioannidis coup sparked the Turkish invasion of northern Cyprus, as a result of which Ioannidis' fellow Colonels promptly withdrew their support, and the junta was forced to bow to both national and international pressure to reinstate parliamentary democracy. Karamanlis was invited to head an interim government, and in the first elections in Greece for over a decade his newly-formed Nea Demokratia (New Democracy) party was voted into power in November 1974.

Modern Politics

Nea Demokratia won the following election in 1977, but was roundly defeated in 1981 by Andreas Papandreou's PASOK. The 1981 election was a true landmark in Greek history, electing the first ever "socialist" government in the history of Greek politics. PASOK won again in 1985, but was defeated by Nea Demokratia in June and November 1989, although both elections were hobbled by a new ruling, passed by PASOK mere months earlier, requiring a 151-seat majority before a party could assume government. A judge, Yannis Grivas, served as a non-partisan interim prime minister until Nea Demokratia finally acquired that majority in 1990, when its new leader, Konstantinos Mitsotakis, duly ousted Papandreou and PASOK. PASOK reversed the voting figures on Nea Demokratia in 1993, with the ailing Papandreou, beset by personal and political controversy, still at its head. Papandreou resigned in 1995, handing the reins to Costas Simitis—noted for introducing the period of *Eksynchronismos* ("modernization") that saw the birth of projects such as the new Venizelos airport, the Athens Metro and the Odos Egnatia superhighway.

Simitis retained his position in the 2000 elections, but the Greeks flipped again in 2004, electing Kostas Karamanlis, Konstantinos' nephew and the new leader of Nea Demokratia. Karamanlis would return to power in the 2007 elections. His opponent was George Papandreou, son of Andreas (who died in 1996, and despite the controversies of his rule attracted an estimated two hundred thousand people to his funeral in Athens). In the 2009 elections George Papandreou reversed the figures on Karamanlis with almost mathematical symmetry, edging slightly ahead of Karamanlis' previous majority, and becoming the third in the successive generations of what is now the Papandreou dynasty to have been prime minister of Greece.

Papandreou, of course, inherited the set of circumstances that tipped Greece into financial chaos in 2010. Despite the criticisms raining down on the Greek political class—and in the absence of a credible alternative—he would appear to have wrought the remarkable feat of making that mythic zone between the rock and the hard place habitable, if not exactly enviable. As Greece contemplates the inevitable fallout from the "default" or debt restructuring of 2011, Papandreou and his party may become casualties of historical circumstance, but that same history may yet acknowledge him as an equal to Trikoupis and Venizelos in the history of remarkable figures in Greece's long and optimistic experiment with democracy.

5 The Written Word
The City in Literature

A thens is too young a city to have accumulated the wrinkles and stains that provide raw material for the writer. Its famous "violet" evening light has exercised poets from Pindar (c. 522-443 BCE) to Palamas (1859-1943) and it has been borrowed by foreign writers from Boccaccio and Chaucer, Shakespeare, Dryden and Milton, the English Romantics (not all of whom were actually able to visit), Melville and Twain, to a flurry of British and American writers in the twentieth century. But apart from producing some of the classical Greek texts, which spent a millennium or so in the safe keeping of Arabic and Latin universities before arriving, translated, in northern Europe in time for the Renaissance, for much of its history Athens was a collection of huts around some fallen architecture and statuary dating from the fifth century BCE—an unlikely source for great or even good literature. It never inspired a *David Copperfield* or a *Nicholas Nickleby*, nor a *Berlin Alexanderplatz* or a *Manhattan Transfer*, although it may well have had its Dickens, Alfred Döblin or its John Dos Passos. It was never a London to inspire a Blake to rail against it, nor did it have a London Bridge for an Eliot to send his crowd flowing across it towards their undoing.

We may also have to consider the possibility, argued by Robin Waterfield, that its greatest Anglophone proselytizers, Byron and Shelley, may in fact have been the willing dupes of the brilliant Hellenic propagandist Adamantios Korais (1744-1833), who cleverly sold the idea of Fair Greece—the term originates in Byron's *Childe Harold's Pilgrimage*—to the Romantics in an early form of viral marketing. Waterfield charges Korais with actually planting the seed of the Fair Greece notion in his own work, knowing that the British would fall for it. Byron fell for it to the extent of proposing

Going viral: Was Byron a willing dupe in Adamantios Korais' scheme?

marriage to a twelve-year-old Athenian girl, Teresa Macri, in his famous "Maid of Athens, ere we part":

> Maid of Athens! I am gone:
> Think of me, sweet! when alone.
> Though I fly to Istambol,
> Athens holds my heart and soul:
> Can I cease to love thee? No!

Despite the offer of an impressive dowry, Teresa's parents turned him down, and Byron anyway had a date with destiny in Messolonghi. The nearest Shelley ever got to Greece was visiting Byron in Venice, but more people remember his "We are all Greeks", from the prologue to his play *Hellas*, than Byron's *Childe Harold's Pilgrimage*, which as well as containing the no less famous "Fair Greece! Sad relic of departed worth!" also contained the more resonant line, "they love thee least who owe thee most". By any reckoning, Adamantios would have considered this ample recompense for his propagandizing efforts.

In fact, it is probably Adamantios whom we have to thank for there being a canon of Greek literature at all. An Enlightenment figure who witnessed the French Revolution, was a friend to Thomas Jefferson and was one of the key intellectual figures of the War of Independence, he launched the Hellenic Library, a seventeen-volume collection of classic texts for the modern Greek reader. As part of his plan to recapture the glory of Periclean Athens (qua-Greece), he also spearheaded the campaign for purist *katharevousa* Greek, which itself would provoke a school of plain, demotic Greek literature in often violent revolt against the elitism of katharevousa.

If we were to attempt to update Korais' canon for modern-day Athens, we would have to extend the city limits to the shores of Turkey and Libya and halfway across the Ionian towards Brindisi in Italy, and for two simple reasons: firstly, until the second half of the nineteenth century, Athens did not have the educated bourgeoisie likely to produce literature. Secondly, even once a literate middle class had developed, many of its greatest figures—not least its two

Nobel laureates, George Seferis (from near Smyrna) and Odysseus Elytis (Heraklion on Crete)—were not born in the city, although like many others they began and continued their careers here. This is also, of course, a crafty journalistic attempt to bend the rules to include writers from outside Athens, but the city was and remains the country's arbiter and clearing house for culture—although I admit I would not want to argue that in a left-wing *kafeneion* in Thessaloniki...

There is also a third reason. Without arguing, if we dare, that these writers were writing in an Athens of the mind, we would lose that quintessential Athenian modernist of his era, Cavafy (born in, died in and hardly left Alexandria during his adult years): sophisticated yet earthed, and that is very much the metaphor we are looking for here, in immemorial Greek literary tradition, but looking to like-minded cities elsewhere in Europe for pointers into the modernist future. We would lose the scandalously untranslated early post-modernist Nikos Gabriel Pentzikis (Thessaloniki), and the first great Greek meta-novelist Stratis Tsirkas (Cairo), too. We would have to send the authors of the National Anthem (Dionysios Solomos, from Zakynthos) and the Olympic Anthem (Kostis Palamas, Patras) back to their villages on the shores of the Ionian. We would probably have to give Adamantios Korais himself a one-way ticket back to Smyrna, as well.

We should also, more seriously, consider a fourth reason: these migrant writers, in a country where geographical mobility is as much a commonplace for bar workers and builders as it is for novelists and poets, would in many cases become bound up in the history of Athens, sometimes even putting themselves, or their civil liberties, on the line to protect (or indeed take over) the city.

Having declared open season on parts of the Mediterranean that were not even Greek less than a century ago, we also have to acknowledge that literary history moved at different speeds in different parts of this new "Greece". While Athens dozed through its millennial siesta, seventeenth-century Crete produced a poet, Vitsentzos Kornaros, and an epic poem, his *Erotokritos*, to rival Chaucer and Boccaccio. There is also a wealth of earlier literature, nowadays largely under lock and key in libraries and museums, dating back into the first millennium and comparable to *Beowulf* and other Early and Middle English texts (and the French Romances and troubadours, too), much of it recorded in the exemplary, if at times eccentric, National Book Centre and Ministry of Culture publication, *Greece: Books and Writers.* Many are also anthologized in the equally exemplary and eccentric *The Greek Poets: Homer to the Present.*

The concept of the "novel" is itself a fairly recent arrival in Greece: while the English language full-length prose-fiction text can be dated back at least to Malory's *Mort d'Arthur* (1485), its Greek equivalent is commonly held to be Emmanuel Roidis' widely-translated *Pope Joan*, from 1866. Roidis was born on Syros, and so Athens could not claim its first true captive novelist until Alexandros Papadiamantis settled there (and he came from Skiathos anyway). Papadiamantis' fiction, such as the novella *The Murderess* (1903) and the stories collected as *Tales from a Greek Island* (1994), treat the condition of his impoverished characters, often from his adopted *yeitoniá* (neighbourhood) of Psirri, in a clear-eyed and unsentimental manner that won him comparisons with Dickens, Dostoevsky, the early Joyce (circa *Dubliners*) and even García Márquez, although an equally clear-eyed reading might more honestly shelve his stories alongside the bittersweet country tales of H. E. Bates.

The novel form is clearly an anomaly in Greek literary history, and would only really get going when Greek writers, like its practitioners elsewhere, were already beginning to dismantle it, in the early twentieth century. The First World War produced the first international Greek bestseller, Stratis Myrivilis' lauded *Life in the Tomb* (1930), and the inter-war years also saw the appearance of Kosmas Politis' *Eroica* (1939), hailed by some as actually superior to the novel that inspired it, Alain-Fournier's *Le Grand Meaulnes*. It would take until 1946 for the appearance of the Big Greek Book, the much-maligned first novel by a nomadic poet then serving in the interim postwar Greek government in Athens, originally titled *The Life and Adventures of Alexis Zorbas*.

If Adamantios Korais and his canon set the meter running on modern Greek and Athenian literature, the period can claim the first great modern Greek poet in the Zakynthian Dionysios Solomos, who was adopted as the nation's poet after his 1823 poem "Hymn to Liberty"—or at least its first two stanzas—became the national anthem, and whose work, most of it published after his death, signalled the revolt against the Enlightenment obsession with archaic katharevousa Greek and established modern, demotic, Greek as the rising literary idiom.

The first great Athenian voice was Kostis Palamas. Trained as a journalist, he later became an administrator of the University of Athens (where nowadays his name graces a building) and published his first collection, *Songs of My Fatherland*, in 1886. He succeeded Solomos in the role of unofficial national poet, not least when he wrote the words to the "Olympic Anthem", first performed at the 1896 Olympics in Athens. He too wrote in demotic Greek and, as our opening quote shows, was not afraid to declare his liberal politics. An ardent modernizer who drew both ire and fire from conservative quarters (he was denounced as a "traitor" in graffiti on the walls of his own university), Palamas' work straddled the old and the new. His first English translator, Aristides Phoutrides, transliterated his Greek into English "thees" and "thous", although these were the mannerisms of a self-confessed admirer of Walt Whitman, rather than the cod-Elizabethan of the Romantics. In collections such as *The Twelve Lays of the Gypsy*, *Life Immovable* and probably his most famous poem "The Palm Tree", Palamas was surveying the landscape that would be inhabited by the likes of Cavafy and Seferis. Athens and Greece appear frequently in his work, the city taking on subtle and modern political roles. His "The Athena Relief", addressed to a carving of the goddess in mournful pose, asks,

I see
Some pain holds Pallas fixed upon
A gravestone. Some great blow moves her:
Is it thy sacred city's loss,
Or seest thou all Greece—alas—
Of now and yesterday entombed?"

Similarly, his "The Palm Tree", ostensibly the poet's transcription of a conversation between some talkative plants and the titular angiosperm, is also rich in metaphoric potential, not least in its vision of "some sunlit Athens" glimpsed in a "sublimer world". Conversely, it could just be a lovely poem about some talking plants.

Palamas was a, if not "the", key figure in Athenian intellectual life for more than thirty years, initially identified with the Greek tendency of the Parnassian school, followers of Théophile Gautier's call for "art for art's sake", and later co-founding the New (or Second) Athenian School, also known as the Palamian School. During the years 1926 to 1940 Palamas was nominated no fewer than fourteen times for the Nobel Prize for Literature, but was passed over (to this day, the Nobel Institute confesses a blind spot towards Greek literature at that time, admitting it also failed to recognize his fellow poet, Angelos Sikelianos).

In the struggle between "pure" katharevousa (seen as the language of jurists and a grammar designed to exclude the uneducated) and "vulgar" demotic Greek, many writers of the late nineteenth-century Athens School adopted traditional folk song and stories as collected by Nikolaos Politis. Others, such as the aforementioned Angelos Sikelianos (born in Lefkada, educated in Athens), sought the sublime in a bridge between classical arts, which Sikelianos celebrated in a short-lived annual festival devoted to what he called the "Delphic Idea", and a modern lyricism of carefully metred and rhymed verse, in works that were compared to Walt Whitman but also presaged the imagery of Seferis and Elytis. Sikelianos had another life as well: a long-standing friend to the novelist Nikos Kazantzakis, he was active in the backrooms of the Greek Resistance, writing the text of a letter that Archbishop Damaskinos sent to the Nazis pleading for the lives of Greece's Jews. He was a strong contender for the 1948 Nobel Prize for Literature, but (and it would appear to have been only after much wrangling) that year's Nobel was awarded to T. S. Eliot.

While a similar battle was engaged in Spain around the same time by writers such as Jiménez and Machado, who looked back to authors such as the sixteenth-century poet Luis de Góngora to find a language that would enable their vision, what makes itself most forcefully felt in this period is the eagerness with which many writers embraced modernism. Most interesting is the under-sung Kostas Karyotakis, although the obvious star from the era is Constantine Cavafy.

International recognition eluded Cavafy during his lifetime, as did any critical airing of the homoerotic content of parts of his work. He was, however, honoured by the Greek state during his lifetime and should soon have a museum dedicated to him in Athens, housed in a mansion in Plaka once occupied by Ioannis Kolettis, prime minister from 1834 to 1835 and 1844 to 1837.

Cavafy's most famous "political" poem, "Waiting for the Barbarians", could have been set in ancient Rome or Romanized Athens (as its "forum" and "senators" seem to imply), but it was clearly intended to be relevant to any city or culture in any age. Similarly, his most famous work, "Ithaka", borrowing Calypso's advice to Odysseus as she frees him and sends him on his way in *The Odyssey*, is not about the island at all, but, perhaps equally obviously, death:

> Keep Ithaka always in your mind.
> Arriving there is what you are destined for.

It is an irony, and one that lends itself to our mischief with maps, that this most far-flung of "Greek" poets was barely known outside the literary Greek middle-class in his lifetime, but became the most famous Greek poet of the twentieth century.

The deeply melancholic Kostas Karyotakis really did try to drown himself in Homer's Ocean, at least the part of it that washes Monolithi beach near his last home, Preveza. Born in Tripoli, in the Peloponnese, he spent a peripatetic childhood as his family moved between the Ionians (Kefallonia, Lefkada) and the mainland (Larissa, Kalamata, Athens) before he became a clerk in local government: a day-job that saw the malcontent poet shunted between various unsatisfactory postings, the last being Preveza, to which he bade a sour farewell in his last ever poem, also titled "Preveza".

Influenced by Baudelaire and other *poètes maudits* as much as by his compatriots, he was initially dismissed as a minor talent, both by the Left and Greek nationalists, but his influence on Greek poetry has grown ever since his tragi-comic suicide, particularly among later Surrealist and avant-garde writers.

His pessimistic tone was leavened with a dark and cynical humour in poems such as "Clerical Workers" and "Ideal Suicides", although he too found the city a source of unexpected lyricism:

> A sweet hour. Athens sprawls like a hetaira
> offering herself to April.
> Sensuous scents are in the air,
> the spirit waits for nothing any more."
>
> ("Athens", 1921)

Despite being an excellent swimmer, as he confessed in his suicide note, he spent ten hours trying to drown himself at Monolithi before abandoning the attempt, buying a gun and shooting himself (bizarrely, his death was recorded in a police "crime scene" photo that survives to this day). His failed attempt to drown himself is imagined in the opening scenes of Tassos Psarras' 2009 television drama series, *Karyotakis*.

Modernists and Surrealists

The supreme Greek modernist, George Seferis, was also born some distance from Athens, in Urla, a town near Smyrna, although his family moved to Athens in 1914. Seferis studied law at the Sorbonne and spent much of his adult life abroad, as a diplomat. He published his first collection, *Strophe*, in 1931, whose longest work, "Erotikos Logos", took forms and themes from Kornaros' *Erotokritos*, but also shared similarities with the French Symbolists. Seferis' eye was also on the future: in 1936 he published the first Greek translation of Eliot's "The Waste Land" (1922), and the poets later became friends. The two have often been compared, particularly in relation to Seferis' own epic, "Mythistorema", published a year earlier, yet although Seferis may have viewed the world through the same appalled lens as Eliot, and employed Eliot's multi-channel technique of "doing the police in different voices" (here, those of Odysseus and Orestes, among others), the poems themselves are worlds apart.

His last posting was as ambassador to London, from which he resigned in 1961. Two years later, "Mythistorema" and later works such as the *Logbooks* won him Greece's first Nobel Prize for Literature, for his "eminent lyrical writing, inspired by a deep feeling for the Hellenic world of culture". In his Nobel acceptance speech on "Modern Greek Tradition" he paid tribute to the likes of Palamas and Solomos, but also acknowledged a debt to Homer and the hero of the Byzantine Cretan epic poem, *Digenis Akritas*.

Seferis used his status to criticize the state of Greek politics, in 1969 issuing a statement on the BBC World Service, copied to every Athens newspaper, attacking the "anomaly" of totalitarian rule, before secluding himself away in what we might see as a symbolic form of self-imposed house arrest. The statement inspired a group of Athenian writers to issue the famous *Eighteen Texts*, a manifesto of human and intellectual liberties, the following year.

The exiled poet Stratis Haviaras (author of two novels of the Second World War and Civil War that truly deserve comparison to Márquez's magic realism, *When the Tree Sings* and *The Heroic Age*) introduced an edition of the *Texts* by describing it as the work of writers "haunted with the same frightening vision: the extinction of the Greek people, or worse, of their humanity". Untold thousands (almost literally: vast crowds flooded the streets, although no one seems to have counted them) attended Seferis' funeral in Athens in 1971, singing Mikis Theodorakis' setting of Seferis' banned poem, "Denial" and turning the funeral into a demonstration against oppression—much as the estimated 100,000 did at Palamas' funeral in the middle of the Nazi occupation. "Denial" is in fact a fairly harmless work, one of many Seferis works banned by the junta, but it struck a chord to the extent that it became the unofficial anthem of the resistance. Only in its third and final stanza does it even begin to hint at just what the culture police feared a metaphor might do in the wrong hands:

> With what spirit, what heart,
> what desire and passion
> we lived our life: a mistake!
> So we changed our life.

Seferis was a leading figure in the Γενιά του '30, or 1930s Generation, along with the younger Odysseus Elytis. Born on Crete but educated in Athens, Elytis was initially regarded as a member of the little-known group of Greek Surrealists (among whom Andreas Embeirikos may prove the most startling discovery for the modern reader) and he associated with figures such as Louis Aragon, André Breton and Tristan Tzara during his four years in Paris in from 1948 to 1952 (he would exile himself there again during the Colonels' regime). But Elytis eschewed Rimbaud's "derangement of the senses" and the automatic writing techniques of the Surrealists for a metaphysics that in his 1959 masterwork, *Axion Esti*—"It is worthy", a phrase from the Orthodox liturgy and also the name of an icon of the Virgin at Athos, which Elytis visited with Nikos Kazantzakis in 1914—entered the realm of the mystical and has been compared to Whitman's *Song of Myself*, not least the pantheism in Whitman's line, "I hear and behold God in every object":

> God my Master Builder, You built me into the mountains,
> God my Master Builder, You enclosed me in the sea!

It also drew on his experience as a soldier fighting the Italians on the Greek-Albanian border at the beginning of the Second World War, and was clearly intended to be read as a work about contemporary as well as ancient Greece. When *Axion Esti* was turned into an oratorio by Mikis Theodorakis in 1960, it was acclaimed as a masterpiece of modern Greek culture. With later works such as *The Monogram* (1972) and *Maria Nephele* (1978), *Axion Esti* won Elytis the 1979 Nobel Prize for Literature.

While Seferis was banned, the poet Yiannis Ritsos lived long enough to be exiled or imprisoned by two different dictatorships, and even saw one of his works, the early collection *Epitaphios* (1936), publicly burned in the shadow of the Acropolis. A communist who later embraced Surrealism, he would be acclaimed as one of the four major Greek poets of the century. He published over a hundred volumes of poetry and was also proposed to the Nobel committee at least seven times.

The largely Athens-based Greek Surrealists are notable partly for their omission from most histories of the movement but also because one of them, Nanos Valaoritis, is still alive and working. Born to Greek parents in Lausanne, Valaoritis was educated in Athens and published his earliest poems, aged eighteen, in the magazine *Ta Nea Grammata* ("The New Writing"), edited by George Katsimbalis, the titular giant of Henry Miller's *The Colossus of Maroussi*. In Athens he fell in with Seferis, Elytis, Miller and Lawrence Durrell, and when Valaoritis was forced to flee occupied Greece he joined Seferis working for the Greek government in exile. Sent to London to enlist British writers to the Greek cause, he also encountered Auden, Eliot and Spender. He returned to Athens after the war but moved to Paris in 1954 with his wife, the Surrealist painter Marie Wilson, be-friending Breton and others in the Surrealist movement. He re-turned to Greece in 1967, but after the Colonels' takeover exiled himself to the USA. He taught for twenty-five years at San Francisco State University, publishing one late prose volume, *My Afterlife Guaranteed*, with City Lights, having been adopted by the likes of Gregory Corso and City Lights founder Lawrence Ferlinghetti. He retired from teaching in 1993 and returned to Greece. His most recent publication was the 2005 collection *Pan Daimonium*, and he continues to edit the literary magazine *Nea Synteleia* (New End of the World).

The Surrealists also have a partial claim on Nikos Gatsos, whose epic poem "Amorgos", said to have been written in a single night's burst of inspiration, is acclaimed as a landmark work of Greek poetry. Gatsos later put aside his poet's pen to write songs with Manos Hadjidakis, who also set parts of the remarkable "Amorgos" to music.

The aforementioned Andreas Embeirikos, by contrast, embraced Rimbaud's voluntary derangement with such enthusiasm that his first work, *Blast Furnace* (1935), was denounced as the work of a heretic and maniac. He was born in Romania but raised in Athens and studied in London and Paris, where he met the Surrealists and psychoanalyst René Laforgue and returned to Athens to practice as Greece's first psychoanalyst, also working at times as a docker in Piraeus. *Blast Furnace* is considered the first Greek Surrealist work, and Embeirikos alternated between work as psychoanalyst and writer through his career, spending decades on the controversial eight-volume novel *O Megas Anatolikos* (Great Eastern), which was only published in 1990. Even today, his work has an incendiary quality that feels as though it could have been written yesterday.

Post-War Writing

The era of Seferis and Elytis saw a new generation of Anglophone writers arriving in Greece, and for entirely different reasons than those that drew the Romantics of the previous century. Patrick Leigh Fermor was headed for Crete, and the war, and his heroic exploits saw him played by Dirk Bogarde in the 1957 Powell and Pressburger film *Ill Met by Moonlight*. He would later, of course, win great acclaim as the revered author of *Mani, Roumeli, A Time of Gifts* and other modern travel classics. (Fermor died in 2011, aged 96, and it is still unknown if he completed the long-promised final book in the *Time of Gifts* trilogy.) His friend Lawrence Durrell headed first for Corfu, where his eve-of-war idyll at Kalami was later recorded in *Prospero's Cell*, and after the war (which he spent in Cairo, working for the British government and starting work on what would become the *Alexandria Quartet*) travelled to Rhodes, captured in *Reflections on a Marine Venus*, finally followed by Cyprus, where his unhappy experiences of both British colonialism and Greek resistance to it produced *Bitter Lemons*. Durrell had already coaxed his friend Henry Miller to Kalami, describing his visit in *Prospero's Cell*, and Miller returned the favour in The *Colossus of Maroussi*, his almost hallucinatory panegyric to Greece, Athens and one Athenian in particular, *Ta Nea Grammata* editor and litterateur-about-town George Katsimbalis. In February 1946 Durrell wrote in elegiac terms about post-war Athens and Katsimbalis:

> Neither Katsimbalis nor Seferis have changed—although the world
> has changed a good deal round them. Athens is unbelievably sad,
> crowded, ill-housed, with money practically worthless and prices
> soaring; and yet in some singular way what they have gone through
> has made them gentle and friendly and sympathetic to each other as
> they never have been before.

Unlike Durrell's work, Miller's book has not weathered the intervening half century well and re-read today lies open to accusa-
tions of bizarre xenophobia (against the British, Americans, the
French and, curiously, in its delirious romanticizing of the Greeks,
even the Greeks themselves) and what might politely be termed
rhapsodic self-absorption. It must have been a swell party, as
recorded in Edmund Keeley's *Inventing Paradise* (1999), although a
younger generation of Greek cultural critics, tooled up with Derrida
and Foucault, is in hot pursuit of the partygoers through the groves
of academe.

The partygoers were perhaps safer out of Greece, where an entirely new mood prevailed among writers after the Civil War. As the
"existentialist" poet Manolis Anagnostakis wrote, this was no time to
be writing poetry about the sea. Anagnostakis was a veteran of both
the wartime Resistance and the Civil War, for which he was tried
and sentenced to death by the post-war government—at the same
time that his anti-Soviet sentiments saw him expelled from the
KKE. The death sentence was commuted to life, and he was released
in 1951 under a new, short-lived, centre-left government. His work,
such as the early *Epoches* and *Synecheia*, was marked by an urgent
epistolary style and an unsparing documentary eye for what was happening to Greece. Despite his dyspeptic worldview, which influenced
later generations of younger writers, Anagnostakis was twice honoured by the government, with a State Poetry Prize in 1985, and a
lifetime achievement National Literature Award in 2002.

The post-war years saw two notable changes in Greek literary
culture, with younger writers adopting the novel form (if only,
perhaps, to bury it, sometimes alive) and also the appearance of more
women writers, a demographic shift due to both the wider availabil-

ity of education and also the stirrings of a nascent women's move-ment. Pioneering women writers such as Melpo Axioti and Dido Sotiriou had been active both in the Greek Left and the publishing world, the former particularly hailed for her avant-garde novel *Twentieth Century* (1946) and the later *Kadmo* (1972), written after her return following decades of political exile. The post-war years witnessed the emergence of writers such as Eleni Vakalo, Kiki Dimoula, Katerina Anghelaki Rooke, Rhea Galanaki, Maria Laina, Pavlina Pampoudi and the prolific Jenny Mastoraki, as well as the novelist and translator Kay Cicellis. Many of these writers are covered in great detail in Karen van Dyck's excellent analytical work, *Kassandra and the Censors*.

The novel, however, was still a male dominated genre, typified by a slew of war and civil war novels, most notably Dimitris Hatzis and his novel *The Defenceless*. This period also produced two of the great-est names in Greek experimental literature: Stratis Tsirkas, and Nikos Gabriel Pentzikis. The former's *Drifting Cities* (a trilogy published between 1961 and 1965) has been compared to Durrell's *Alexandria Quartet*, while Pentzikis' *Architecture of a Dissipated Life* (1963), a dis-cursive anti-novel dedicated to the avoidance of its own narrative, issued fair warning about a talent who has been championed by the French (in particular, admirers of Georges Perec) but whose novels (*Archive, The Novel of Mrs Ersi, Mother Thessalonica, The Dead Man and the Resurrection*) are scandalously unavailable in English trans-lation.

The two most successful novels of the post-war era are better known for the films that propelled them on to the international scene, although it is worth betting that they would have made it there themselves anyway. Nikos Kazantzakis' first novel, better known nowadays simply as *Zorba the Greek* (1946), was in fact published some time after the work that had already won him a place in Greek literary history, his *The Odyssey: A Modern Sequel* (1936), an epic of exactly 33,333 lines of verse (as opposed to the original's 12,110 lines) imagining Odysseus leaving Ithaca again, this time on a voyage of self-discovery in which he encounters Don Quixote, the Buddha and Jesus. *Zorba* itself has been unfairly shackled to a popular cultural cliché about Greece, thanks largely to a dance that Anthony Quinn improvised to a ditty concocted by Mikis Theodorakis, although it is a cliché easily undone: in both book and film, not once will you see a plate being smashed to the accompaniment of a bouzouki.

Vassilis Vassilikos' 1967 novel *Z*, an imaginative response to the assassination of politician Grigoris Lambrakis, became an international bestseller and was translated into more than thirty languages. It was actually Vassilikos' debut, written in exile during the Colonels' regime, and he has written dozens of others, few of them translated into English (his most recent English-language publication, *The Few Things I Know About Glafkos Thrassakis*, published in 2003, is a satire of literary stardom written in 1979). We considered the political events around the Lambrakis murder earlier, and re-visit Costa-Gavras' film in the next chapter, but Vassilikos' novel itself is one of those urgent, angry works that manage to touch a nerve and, if not quite effect change, then speak, as another cliché goes, truth to power. Vassilikos continues to write, but is nowadays also Greece's ambassador to UNESCO.

Vassilikos is a member of what the collective authors of *Greece: Books* call "the WWII Generation"—writers born and brought up during both Nazi occupation and the turbulence of civil war, but dealing with life after, in a Greece rebuilt by the Marshall Plan, diaspora billionaire remittances, the urban planning of fascist dictatorships and socialist ideologues. Curiously, many writers have taken to an extremely popular genre in Greece, the thriller (perhaps for the same reasons that Borges found it so rich in allegorical potential), most notably in Antonis Samarakis' international bestseller *To Lathos* (1965), translated as "The Flaw" but more accurately titled "The Mistake". Both Menis Koumandareas and Costas Taktsis combined literary achievement with popular success, the former with novels such as the powerful novella *Koula* (1978), *H faneia me tou ennia* (1986), filmed as *Vest Number Nine* by director Pantelis Voulgaris, and *Their Smell Makes Me Cry* (1996), and the latter most famously with his 1967 novel, *The Third Wedding*, a bestseller in translation shortly before his death in 1988.

A younger generation is still busy inventing new ways to write in what we might call the post-modern Athens. Amanda Michalopoulou, who has described herself as a psychogeographer of her city, has, in novels such as *I'd Like* (2008), found an urban Greek voice that might be compared to Joan Didion, although she is more frequently compared to Borges and Calvino, and the narrative mischief of *I'd Like* deserves comparison to the best of Robert Coover. Ersi Sotiropoulos found herself the centre of a new protest movement when over forty other writers launched a petition of support after her fifth novel, the controversial moral fable, *Zig-Zag through the Bitter-Orange Trees* (2006), was melodramatically withdrawn from school libraries because of its content. And we can sleep content that the Greek avant-garde is alive and well in at least the person of Dimitris Lyacos, whose extraordinary *Poena Damni* trilogy, *First Death* (1996), *Nyctivoe* (2001) and *Z213: EXIT* (2005), combines the scarier hallucinations of William Burroughs with the paranoid narratives of Kafka or Beckett, harking back to Dante but also forward into experimental speculative prose.

Greece has a small population (barely eleven million) for which it produces fewer than (from official 2008 figures) ten thousand native publications a year. Britain, by comparison, produces around ten times as many for only six times the population. The maths might suggest Greeks read less, but this is skewed by the predominance of foreign language bestsellers (led by the ubiquitous Dan Browns and Stieg Larssons) over a small but energetic indigenous publishing industry, which subsidizes homegrown talent by publishing translations of the Browns and Larssons. In 2008 one of Athens' many innovative domestic publishing houses scored an international success that fell like a gift into the lap of this project. Simply put, there can be no better book to close a summary of Athenian and Greek literature.

Apostolos Doxiadis and Christos H. Papadimitrious' graphic novel *Logicomix* (2008) added the *Financial Times* Books of the Year and *Publishers Weekly* Books of 2009 to its number one listing in the *New York Times* bestsellers lists, and so far has been translated into twenty-two languages, including Finnish, French, German, Italian, Mandarin and Turkish. A "literary" graphic novel in the tradition of

Art Spiegelman's *Maus*, it is the story-within-a-story of the authors' attempts to explain the work of the great mathematician and philosopher Bertrand Russell, with the help of graphic artists Alecos Papadatos and Annie Di Donna, all of whom appear in the opening pages (and in a house by the Acropolis) and re-appear to comment on the work at later points. (Doxiadis, also known as a dramatist and filmmaker, addressed similar philosophical concerns in his earlier novel *Uncle Petros and Goldbach's Conjecture*, one of so far four conventional novels he has also published.) The cinematic devices continue through their exploration of Russell's life and work, employing split-screens, interior monologue, German Expressionist camera angles and film noir lighting, flashbacks and to-camera asides (if this book were a movie, the name on the front would be either Godard or Resnais). With walk-on parts for Kurt Gödel, Alan Turing and Ludwig Wittgenstein, as well as Aeschylus and Aristotle, this clever post-modern comic caper, embracing the history of philosophy from Aristotle's *Organon* to Wittgenstein's *Tractatus Logico-Philosophicus*, became an unlikely bestseller in numerous languages. And amusingly, despite Doxiadis and Papadimitrious' joke about Henry Miller and the Acropolis, it actually begins in the Acropolis gardens, and ends in the Theatre of Dionysus, next door, although, like all movie blockbusters, this denouement appears to be setting up the viewer to buy tickets for the sequel, nothing less than a book-length cartoon strip explaining the birth of Athenian democracy.

6 | Visual Images
Art, Cinema and Drama

Between the antiquities of the Acropolis and the modern collections of the National and Contemporary Art museums, there is a vast gap in the history of art in Athens and Greece that was only closed by the opening of the Athens School of Fine Arts in 1837. While the Byzantine era left the city with numerous churches crammed with Byzantine art, Athens was sidelined through its centuries of Ottoman rule, unperturbed by the Renaissance and untouched by either the Cretan or Ionian Schools, the latter largely influenced by Italian art imported by the Venetians who ruled parts of the archipelago between the thirteenth and nineteenth centuries.

Athens acquired its first indigenous art movement with the advent of the Munich School, a late nineteenth-century group of Greek painters identified historically by their attendance at the Royal Academy of Fine Arts in Munich. We have already encountered the most famous member, Theodoros Vryzakis, whose Romantic influence reached its peak in his 1853 *The Exodus from Missolonghi*, in which God and a host of angels look down from the clouds on the famous War of Independence siege. This and his *The Bishop of Old Patras Germanos Blesses the Flag of Revolution* were accomplished and shameless fabrications on behalf of the New Athens propaganda office, managing to serve both the mythology of the new nation and the almost instantaneous nostalgia for a revolution that did not actually happen quite like that.

Vryzakis' fellow Müncheners such as Nikiphoros Lytras and Nikolaos Gyzis also mixed Romantic archetypes with nationalist symbolism, although the latter, skilled in a variety of styles, echoed both Caravaggio and Goya while also prefiguring Impressionism and art nouveau. It took a later generation of painters such as Georgios Chatzopoulos, Georgios Iakovidis, Periklis Pantazis and Pavlos

Frieze frame: Sculptor Costas Varotsos' second, larger, *Dromeas (Runner)* flees the Hilton

Leonidas Drosis' sculpture of Athena atop an Ionic column outside the Academy (*top left*); the Arch of Hadrian with the Acropolis framed beyond (*top right*); Edward Dodwell's 1821 painting of the Turkish settlement around the west side of the Parthenon, which was then largely the extent of the inhabited city (*below*)

The Thiseion, or Hephaisteion, now framed by gardens, but in 1870 it was still surrounded by a desert of prickly pear (*above*). Parliament building in Syntagma Square, built in 1843 as the Royal Palace, now with the art deco Tomb of the Unknown Soldier below it and snow on Mount Hymettus beyond (*below*)

A frieze from the Parthenon Marbles at the British Museum (*left*); some very expensive urban sprawl in Kolonaki (Voukourestiou is somewhere down there) (*below*); the National Library on Panepistimiou, with Panayis Vallianos on his plinth (*bottom*)

Freedom or death: Theodoros Vryzakis' 1865 painting, *The Bishop of Old Patras Germanos Blesses the Flag of Revolution*, now thought to be an imaginative work of revolutionary propaganda conflating several events into one iconic image

Eleftherios Venizelos gazes out of a 1920s map drawing on Rhigas Velestinlis' *Charta* map of a Greater Greece (*above*). Ernst Ziller's Megas Alexandros and (left) Bagkeion Megaron hotels await renovation on Omonia Square (*below*)

Nobel laureate and occasional haiku writer George Seferis (*top left*); Dimitris Lyacos, cartographer of new maps of hell (*top right*); Amanda Michalopoulou, whose work has been compared to Calvino and Coover (*left*)

True Athenians at the Acropolis: *Logicomix* authors Papadimitriou and Doxiadis set out on their search for the essence of Bertrand Russell, captured in stop-frame from a crane-cam imagined by artists Annie Di Donna and Alecos Papadatos

A classic Theo Angelopoulos set piece, the waterborne funeral sequence from his *Trilogy: The Weeping Meadow* (*above*), while the shark from *Jaws* is about to make an unexpected appearance in Yorgos Lanthimos' dark modern fable *Dogtooth* (*below*)

Mina Orfanou crosses the gender divide as Panos Koutras' titular *Strella* (*above*), while Evangelia Randou and Ariane Labed act up in Athina Rachel Tsangari's *Attenberg* (*right*). Takis' *Signals* sculptures take a sighting on the Arc de Triomphe (*bottom left*), and Nikos Hadjikyriakos-Ghika dismantles the Athens skyline (*bottom right*)

The National Theatre of Greece (*top left*), and the Bios roof terrace at night (*top right*); Giannis Nikolaidis as Jason sets sail across Dimitris Papaioannou's waterlogged *Medea*² set (*above*). Panathinaikos play the OAKA Stadium (*below left*); the former gasworks of Technopolis light up (*below right*)

(*Clockwise from top left*) Savina Yannatou, mapping a universe of Mediterranean musics; Iannis Xenakis, the great twentieth century Greek avant-garde composer; the National Observatory from the Pnyx hill; Exarheia Square; Stereo Nova, the missing link between Kraftwerk and *rebetiko*; Manos Hadjidakis would have defied the smoking ban

The Mall Athens architecture echoes the shapes of Santiago Calatrava's nearby Olympic arches (*above*), while Manolis Anastasakis' West Athens Towers proposal took the olive leaf as the model for his triple whorled "multiskyscraper" (*left*). The Varvakeios Market on Athinas, best avoided when Athenians descend on it to stock up for holidays and holy days (*opposite top*); a spice stall outside the market (*opposite bottom*)

"He was only fifteen…" The monument to Alexandros Grigoropoulos, on the corner of Mesolongiou and Tzavella streets, the latter now renamed Alexis Grigoropoulos Street, in Exarheia (*above*). The aftermath of the Grigoropoulos riots (*below*)

The National Gardens, a small green lung at the heart of the city, just a few metres from Syntagma Square (*above*). The prize-winning Hollwich Kushner "windscraper" proposal for the derelict Piraeus Tower site (*below*)

Into the sunset: Acropolis and Piraeus, the rock's likely destination in another sixty million years, if plate tectonics don't tug the city beneath the waves (*above*). The ultimate Athens suburb, Hydra, once a bohemian hideout for Leonard Cohen and a subaquatic Sophia Loren, today marketed as the "Hellenic Hamptons" (*below*)

Kalligas—Athenian students of the Munich generation—to start addressing the Greek landscape itself, although representation was already dissolving towards abstraction with techniques clearly borrowed from the likes of Cézanne and Monet. With Greek Impressionism under full sail around the turn of the century, painters including Nikolaos Lytras, trained by his father Nikiphoros at the School of Fine Arts, Konstantinos Maleas and Konstantinos Parthenis made a uniquely Greek form of Impressionism, whose minimal land- and seascapes could be seen as a visual prefiguring of the poetry of Seferis and others.

Modernism and Since

The city and country found its first genius in Nikos Hadjikyriakos-Ghika. He studied in Paris and also under the great Greek modernist Dimitris Galanis, absorbing both Constructivism and Cubism and offering one of the first avant-garde visions of the city itself in his *Athens Houses* of 1928. He also applied the Cubist's prism to street scenes of Athens, the suburb of Kifissia, numerous landscapes of Hydra and elsewhere. Hadjikyriakos-Ghika now has his own dedicated museum, in his former home in an apartment block on Kriezotou Street off Panepistimiou (the Syntagma end), administered by the Benaki.

The Athens branch of the Surrealist movement, while largely remembered as a literary circle, also included a number of accomplished painters, including Nikos Engonopoulos who, as well as producing written texts, painted Surrealist works in the manner of Max Ernst. The city also weighed into the abstract movement early on, with painters such as Alekos Kontopoulos and sculptors including Memos Makris, famous for his memorial to the dead at Mauthausen concentration camp and his memorial to the 1973 student uprising in the form of a gigantic head of a youth in the grounds of the Athens Polytechnic, and Thodoros Papadimitriou, noted for his droll constructions suspended from bicycle wheels balanced on tightrope-like wires. And although it stretches to breaking point even our lax geographical grasp of "Athens", we should also note the work of Theodoros Stamos: born in Manhattan to Greek parents, later self-exiled in some disgrace to Lefkada, but frequently exhibited in Athens in later life, Stamos was one of the core eighteen "Irascibles", as *Time* dubbed them, of the 1940s Abstract Expressionist movement, when he was barely into his twenties. The "disgrace" came through Stamos' role in the scandal over the estate of Mark Rothko in the 1970s, when Rothko's executors were found guilty of manipulating the market in Rothko works. Stamos was forced to sign over his house, then worth a remarkable half a million dollars, to the Rothko family. At first influenced by the likes of William Baziote, his later works can compare to the colour-field pieces of Clyfford Still and Barnett Newman.

Others went in the other direction to reclaim representation, in particular Yannis Tsarouchis, born in Piraeus and an accomplice of Matisse and Giacometti during a short spelling living in Paris in the early 1930s. He returned to Greece in 1936 and started producing landscapes, still lifes and portraits that are regarded as among the most important of the "Thirties Generation". Even though the police once tore down one of his paintings in an exhibition at the Zappeion Hall, throughout his career he produced endearingly chaste homo-erotic groups of sailors and soldiers, and tenderly erotic images of semi-naked young men, often blessed with either angelic or butter-fly wings. His house in the northern suburb of Maroussi is now a museum to his work, although it is unlikely that Henry Miller ever visited it.

Despite war, famine and insurrection, Athens seethed with talent in the mid twentieth century, perhaps most famously the enduring young rebel sculptor Takis (Panayiotis Vassilakis), born here in 1925 and still planting suspect devices in public spaces. Takis, as he is singularly known throughout Greece and beyond, started making sculptures inspired by Picasso and Giacometti, entirely self-taught, in his teens. In the mid-1950s, based in Paris, he began the lifelong *Signals* series—tall, spindly outdoor kinetic sculptures that produced sounds either when the wind blew them together, or, later, by magnetic or electronic means. His often menacing works, usually affixed to the points of slender upright industrial screws, have sprouted in plazas and water gardens across the world, and supplied the soundtracks to a production of Sophocles' *Electra* at Epidaurus and also Costa-Gavras' 1975 film, *Section Spéciale*. Still disturbing the neighbours in his eighties, Takis' work with sculpture and noise has a fascinating overlap with the work of composer Iannis Xenakis, and also the younger sonic terror Coti K, both of whom we encounter in the next chapter.

Athens also had its Pop movement, notably with the former Surrealist turned pop self-publicist Yiannis Gaitis, who transformed his ubiquitous bowler-hatted homunculus figure into an icon almost as familiar as Warhol's soup can, reproducing it in friezes, sculptures, themed merchandise and even hotel décor reproductions. Greek Pop art also parried the minimalism of Sol LeWitt and Bruce Nauman in the works of (among others) Chryssa Vardea, the first Greek artist to work with neon and also noted for her pieces using paper, typography, industrial and street signage.

Athens today can sometimes seem awash with young artists whose work outpaces that of contemporaries in Berlin, London, New York, Paris and elsewhere. At the upper end of the market, it recently acquired a branch of New York dealer Larry Gagosian's Gagosian Gallery (tucked, in fact, just behind the Benaki) and it is also home to Athens' answer to the Saatchi Gallery, the DESTE Foundation, owned by the billionaire art collector Dakis Joannou. Nowadays housed in a former sock factory in Nea Ionia (a trek out there on the Metro, and another through the suburban wilderness of Nea Ionia itself, is worth it, if only after checking the website for opening hours), DESTE is a mini-Hermitage of contemporary art of the sort that could only be indulged by a multi-billionaire property and construction magnate. Joannou, who is said to refuse to sell any of his acquisitions, is an avid collector of Jeff Koons, Maurizio Cattelan, Damien Hirst, Jean-Michel Basquiat, Chris Ofili and many others. Joannou and his curators have also exhibited older, established, names, including Beuys, Duchamp, Man Ray, Francis Picabia and Ed Ruscha, and of the five-hundred-plus artists showcased by DESTE in the past decade around half are Greeks, including the lauded sculptor Dora Economou, Jannis Kounellis, whose found-object *arte povera* constructions are in the Tate collection, and

Lefteris Yakoumakis, one of the new "irascibles" of the Greek branch of the Stuckist tendency.

At the funkier, opposite end of the market there is any number of artists and gallerists who would cheerfully burn down DESTE. Some, such as the guerrilla video artist Miltos Manetas and the conceptual artist-architect Andreas Angelidakis, straddle both DESTE and downtown, while others are the impossibly hip underground who took to the streets for the two Athens Biennale events so far, *DESTROY ATHENS* in 2007, and *HEAVEN*, in 2009, with another threatened in 2011.

In between is a thriving circuit of galleries large and small, private and state owned, some sponsored by banks and corporations, others just bars or warehouse spaces hidden in the backstreets of Exarheia, Gazi and beyond. Inside them is the art of a bewildering array of young and not-so-young artists, whose numbers simply cannot equate with the rude mathematics of the Greek education system. And the Athens art scene has yet to fall victim to curatorial megalomania, rapacious galleries charging artists fifty per cent commission and media mafias driving meaningless trends, all of which plague its London and New York counterparts. Athenians themselves just cannot get enough of their artists. And sometimes, it seems, the weirder, the better.

Filming Athens

Cinema was in one of the rear cars on the same rollercoaster that the arts in Greece rode through the wars, dictatorships and democracies of the twentieth century. Unlike the other arts, however, it lent itself to two forms: films made by Greeks, and films made in Greece. The latter is a largely dismal genre, bookended, at least in English-speaking terms, by *Summer Holiday* (1963) and Jonathan Nossiter's art-house thriller, *Signs & Wonders* (2000). The former, a pre-counter-cultural youth musical vehicle for Cliff Richard, which features the singer driving a London bus around Syntagma Square and his band, The Shadows, performing in front of the Parliament dressed as Evzone guards, might possibly be due a post-modern re-appraisal as camp. Nossiter's lo-tech art house mystery, applying pop video techniques to a thriller set in the streets of Athens, made under the sign of Nicolas Roeg and with an eye on the narrative devices of Michael Haneke, is proof that forty years after *Don't Look Now* it is no longer possible to make a convincing psychological mystery in which the killer is a small person in a red raincoat.

Greek films by Greek filmmakers flourished in the "Golden Age" of the 1950s and 1960s, although capital and country have a film history tracking back into the last years of the nineteenth century (as we will see, some filmmakers are busy excavating this history). We might date the Golden Age from the debut by Michael Cacoyannis, *Windfall in Athens* (1954), a romantic comedy revolving around the device of a stolen lottery ticket. Like many of these earlier films, it was shot against an Athens that has vanished from landscape and memory and resides now only in obscure archives. Born in Cyprus, Cacoyannis was actually raised in London and only moved to Athens after his debut was a success—one that enabled him to embark on his first major project, the aforementioned *Stella* (1955), which won Cacoyannis his first award, a Golden Globe for Best Foreign Film. Melina Mercouri, as the vivacious sex bomb of the title, got a better press than the director, hinting at the other sex bomb she would portray, Ilya, in *Never on Sunday* (1960), which won her an Oscar nomination and a Best Actress Award at Cannes that year. Director and soon-to-be husband Jules Dassin played the Henry Higgins character (here excruciatingly renamed "Homer Thrace") to her Eliza Doolittle in this Piraeus-set reworking of the Pygmalion legend, in which the footage of an early low-rise Piraeus is almost as fascinating as their comical romance. The film also gave the world Manos Hadjidakis' song "Ta paidia tou Peiraia" ("The Kids of Piraeus"), better known as "Never on Sunday", the first foreign-language composition to win an Academy Award for Best Original Song, and one that was covered around the globe in twelve different languages, including Mandarin, and became a dancefloor remix hit in 2010.

Another famous piece of music, this time by Mikis Theodorakis, dogs Cacoyannis' enduring masterpiece, *Zorba the Greek* (1964), and even though it is set on Crete it does at least, for the requirements of our subject, start in a grimly rainy Piraeus. Cacoyannis pursued this dour tone throughout his unvarnished monochrome tale of small village spite, illumined only by the bookish Alan Bates' adventures with the cheery existential clown Anthony Quinn. It was nominated for seven Oscars, but that year *My Fair Lady* swept the board, leaving it with just three: cinematography, art direction and Supporting Actress, for Lila Kedrova. Strangely, while director Cacoyannis (Cypriot) and his stars Bates (English), Kedrova (Russian) and Quinn (Mexican) were all Oscar-nominated, the one Greek lead, the statuesque Irene Papas, was not. It would also seem that the counter-rumour that Quinn invented Zorba's dance on the spot due to a broken ankle is itself an urban myth: no one can move like that on broken bones. That contra-myth planted, the film remains a handsome achievement nearly half a century on, and neither it, nor its title, deserves the pejorative associations acquired over the decades.

The other cinematic landmark from this era is Nikos Koundouros' *O Drakos* ("The Dragon", aka "The Ogre of Athens", 1956), voted number one in a 2006 Greek Film Critics Association poll of the ten best Greek movies ever made. (Curiously, it also crops up as a trope in Jonathan Franzen's novel, *Freedom*.) Shot in shadowy noir/expressionist monochrome, and set mostly in a wild *Cubanismo-meets-rebetiko* nightclub, it is a visual feast of a film in which a timid clerk is mistaken for the titular underworld killer, finds he rather likes the gangster lifestyle, but is exposed, with unhappy consequences. The film has some unusual historical notes attached. Koundouros and actor Thanasis Veggos (Spathis the barman) first met when both were prisoners in the post-Civil War government's concentration camp on the island of Makronisos in the 1950s. Veggos went on to become a much-loved comic actor, and was mourned as a national hero when he died aged 83 in 2011. In 1995 he took a cameo role as Harvey Keitel's taxi driver in Theo Angelopoulos' *Ulysses' Gaze*, in which Angelopoulos sends Keitel's character, the filmmaker known simply as "A", in search of lost footage from *The Weavers*, the early (1905) documentary by Macedonian film pioneers the Manaki brothers.

Cacoyannis began the 1960s with his acclaimed version of Euripides' *Electra* (1962), the first in a trilogy of works derived from

Euripides followed by *The Trojan Women* in 1971 and *Iphigenia* in 1977, all three starring Irene Papas with soundtracks by Mikis Theodorakis. He also, in the many years he spent working in theatre and opera, produced dramatic and operatic versions of *The Bacchae*, *Iphigenia in Tauris* and *Medea*. In 1967, however, Cacoyannis joined the exodus following the Colonels' coup.

Costa-Gavras (born Konstantinos Gavras) had been based in Paris since 1951, as his father's involvement with the wartime liberation movement EAM and subsequent jailing for suspected communist sympathies blocked Costa-Gavras from the Greek higher education system and also from studying in the USA. In France he worked as an assistant to René Clair, among others, and directed his first film, *The Sleeping Car Murders*, a noirish thriller, in 1965, followed by the French Resistance drama, *One Man Too Many*, in 1967. The same year, the Athenian journalist Vassilis Vassilikos, forced into exile because of his political activities, published his first novel, *Z*, in France. Based on the 1963 assassination of liberal-left politician Grigoris Lambrakis, *Z* was an almost impossibly timely literary debut in the year of the Colonels' takeover, and with the Spanish novelist, Jorge Semprún, Costa-Gavras set about turning it into a film. The film was shot in Algeria, as Greece was off-limits to the filmmakers, and won the Oscar for Best Foreign Film in 1970, its first year of Oscar eligibility after its release in 1969.

Thanks perhaps partly to its director's grounding in the French *nouvelle vague*, and a heavyweight cast of Yves Montand, Irene Papas and Jean-Louis Trintignant, it established Costa-Gavras as a master of the political thriller and remains a classic of the genre. Costa-Gavras lost friends on the Left with his subsequent *The Confession* (1971), a similar critique of communist totalitarianism, but this was only the beginning of a career in which he turned a non-partisan eye on crooked juntas of any shade across the world, in films such as *State of Siege* (1972) and *Missing* (1982). In 2008 he returned to his birthplace to start work on what was ironically his first film made there, *Eden is West* (2009), a tragicomedy about stateless migrants landing in Greece and hoping to make their way to the paradise (*paradeisos* in the original Greek title) of the West, Paris.

Not everyone left in 1967, however. Some stayed to argue, or work the system, or simply lacked the wherewithal to flee. Theo Angelopoulos chose, almost perversely, to remain in the city where he was born (later hymning it in the little-seen documentary, *Athens, Return to the Acropolis*), spurred into staying and taking a job as film critic with the left-wing daily, *Allagi*, after a run-in with the authorities reminded him of his priorities. *Allagi* was later closed by the junta, but Angelopoulos was already working on his own film projects, starting with an aborted rockumentary about the Greek rock band Forminx. Angelopoulos completed his first short, *Broadcast*, a witty dismantling of media celebrity that un-cannily prefigures the era of reality television, in 1968. His first full-length feature, *Reconstruction* (1970), set out the Angelopoulos stall, a murder thriller in which chronology and reality become malleable in the hands of the capricious *auteur* director. Cannily, Angelopoulos showed the film to the critics before he let the censors see it, and the immediate acclaim forestalled any moves by the junta to edit or ban it. Similar games with the censors enabled him to film the follow-up, the complex political hostage drama *Days of '36* (1972), in places he told one interviewer he would not have been allowed to film even after the junta fell. He then set off around the country with cast and crew to film the four-hour mas-terpiece that made his name, *The Travelling Players* (1975), which harvested a crop of international awards, including the International Critics' Award at Cannes and Film of the Year at the British Film Institute awards.

The players are members of an itinerant theatre troupe, slogging through the hinterland in the years 1939 to 1952 with a production of the popular folk romance *Golfo the Shepherdess*, by no coincidence the subject of the first ever Greek feature film, made by Costas Bachatoris in 1914. The players are named after members of the mythic Atreides clan (Agamemnon, Clytemnestra, Electra and so on), and these figures stand in for the warring factions in the troupe as the director cycles through the years of war, famine, civil war, democracy and dictatorship. What made the film a *film*, however, was Angelopoulos' work with his cinematographer Giorgos

Arvanitis, who shot every Angelopoulos film up to and including *Eternity and a Day* (2002). *The Travelling Players* used fewer than eighty shots, some as long as five minutes, during its almost four hour duration, which was spellbinding for many but for others it was almost unwatchably long.

Angelopoulos and Arvanitis are renowned for their majestic set pieces, like vast nineteenth-century landscape paintings: a gigantic marble hand being winched out of the sea and into the sky above Thessaloniki (*Landscape in the Mist*, 1988), a wedding that has to be conducted across a flooded border river in winter, with bride and groom, guests and just one priest separated on either bank, hiding from the passing border patrols (*The Suspended Step of the Stork*, 1991), or an enormous statue of Lenin, being transported on a barge drifting down a river (*Ulysses' Gaze*, 1995)—although the small poetry of their shots of empty country roads, forlorn railway stations and blasted, tundra-like landscapes is equally vivid. With later films such as *Eternity and a Day* and the most recent *The Dust of Time* (2008) there has been a temptation to read Angelopoulos' often stellar male leads (Willem Dafoe, Bruno Ganz, Harvey Keitel) as ciphers for the director: filmmakers or writers on a Homeric quest through a Greece or some Balkan no-man's-land as mysterious and threatening as the Zone in Andrei Tarkovsky's *Stalker*.

The films became conventionally shorter, but the backlash was quick in arriving: as early as 1979, Angelopoulos noted with some pique to one interviewer, the Thessaloniki Film Festival slugged "Death to Angelopoulos!" on its posters. An ironic usage, no doubt, probably a posture struck by film theorists who prefer a little more Godard in their movie fare, but it did signal a general impatience with a filmmaker who had became a national institution and perhaps as frozen as his magnificent cinematic visions. There is a politics in Angelopoulos' films, from the thrillers to the existential explorations of identity and belonging in the later works (this is, after all, a man who studied with Claude Lévi-Strauss at the Sorbonne), but it was probably inevitable that a more radical younger generation weaned on cheap hand-held cameras and pop-video editing techniques would relegate him to the old guard. It is unlikely that Angelopoulos is perturbed, with a body of work that continues to grow and is frequently compared to that of Terrence Malick—but probably more deserves comparison to cinematic poet-philosophers such as Tarkovsky or Victor Erice. His films also have a deeper political resonance not always visible at the time of their release: the wedding in *Suspended Step of the Stork* was shot on the same river, the Evros, where Greece is currently building its controversial anti-immigrant fence.

Other mavericks also stayed behind and operated below the wire, not least Alexis Damianos, whose most famous film, *Evdokia* (1971), was voted the greatest Greek film ever in a 1986 poll, and came just second to *O Drakos* in that 2006 critics' top ten. His earlier *Before the Ship Sails* (1968) was a neo-realist tale of a shepherd's attempt to leave his pastures and emigrate to Australia, but *Evdokia* might better be compared to the brutalism of a Fassbinder in its bleak portrayal of an ill-starred love affair between a prostitute and a career army officer.

Modern Trends

Television arrived in Greece in 1971, and hammered its film industry. Prior to its arrival, cinema attendances had reached 180 million a year; afterwards, they slumped to just seventy million and continued downwards. Funding evaporated and the big names stayed in exile. The "New Greek Cinema" percolated in the new film schools, but few managed to turn their evident talent into box office takings. As the radical critic Dan Georgakas saw it, "a persistent problem for them was that their political positions impelled them to seek a mass audience while their aesthetics often drove that audience away." A notable, almost singular, exception to this is Pantelis Voulgaris, whose films, from *The Engagement of Anna* (1972) to his international hit *Brides* (2004) and the recent *Deep Soul* (2009), won awards and audiences without compromising their integrity.

The situation began to shift in 1981, when the government launched the Greek Film Center, to promote and fund Greek cinema, although a recent spat between the newly-formed FoG (Filmmakers of Greece) and the government suggests that things have yet to improve. FoG claims that the government funding system has become complacent and hidebound, funding a small coterie of established names and ignoring new (or, indeed, old) talent. It also charges that the government has failed to deliver promised funding for new Greek films. This is doubly ironic at a time when an even newer new wave of young Greek (and largely Athenian) filmmakers is suddenly taking the world, or at least its film festivals, by storm, including Panos Koutras' *Strella* (2009), Yorgos Lanthimos' *Dogtooth* (2009), Athina Rachel Tsangari's *Attenberg* (2010) and Filippos Tsitos' *Plato's Academy* (2010).

Koutras' *Strella* is a poignant gender-tangle romance between an ex-con and a transvestite hooker, comparable perhaps to Almodóvar. It follows his earlier *Real Life* (2004), a David Lynch-like surreal melodrama in which Koutras pictured the Acropolis in flames, and his Science Fiction spoof, *Attack of the Giant Moussaka* (1999), a cult at film festivals around the world and far superior to its obvious titular inspiration, *Attack of the Killer Tomatoes*. *Dogtooth*, a stylish if dark modern fairy story, part comedy, part shocker, about a father who keeps his children locked away from the real world, was the Greek submission for the 2010 Best Foreign Language Film at the Oscars. (Lanthimos lost, but *Dogtooth* was the first Greek film to be chosen for nomination by the Oscars committee in thirty-three years, since Cacoyannis' *Iphigenia* in 1977.) Tsangaris' *Attenberg*, which takes its title from a character's mis-hearing of the surname of the famous zoologist Sir David, and applies his methodologies to two young women growing up strange in a strange seaside town, won one of its leads, Ariane Labed, the Best Actress award at the 2010 Venice Film Festival. Tsitos' *Plato's Academy* is a sharp satire on Greek xenophobia, planting the unsayable in the mouths of a group of shopkeepers bickering on an Athens street corner.

Evidence there alone of a strong breeze blowing through new Greek cinema. There has also been a marked rise in the number of young Greek women filmmakers, not least from director-producer Tsangaris, but also, following earlier Greek New Wave veterans such as Tonia Marketaki and Frieda Liappa, younger directors including Angeliki Antoniou (*Donusa*, 1992, and the recent, award-garlanded,

Eduart, 2007), Kleoni Flessa (*Let's Go for an Ouzo*, 2002), and Marsa Makris (*Dry Cleaning*, 2005). There are similar signs of revival in the Greek art movie, particularly in the work of Angelos Frantzis, an assistant director on *Ulysses' Gaze*, whose *A Dog's Dream* (2004) opens with a dizzyingly long hand-held tracking shot that glides into a sleek noir thriller, and whose most recent *In the Woods* (2010) is a filmic tone poem shot on an off-the-shelf pocket video camera to rich, Jarman-esque, effect.

While the Greek multiplex circuit is dominated by Hollywood blockbusters and Greek-themed sex comedies such as *The Kings of Mykonos* (in fact, an Australian production funded by Paramount, and so cheerfully crass it makes *Driving Aphrodite* look like a Merchant-Ivory period piece), it is left to poorly funded organizations such as the Greek Film Center to struggle to preserve a fast-disappearing Greek film history. One name that deserves greater exposure is that of the late Stavros Tornes, whose eerie mystery fable *Karkalou* (1984) was number ten in the 2006 critics' all-time bests list. Tornes worked on *Zorba the Greek* and Elia Kazan's *America, America* (1963), but fled Greece after the Colonels' takeover, returning in secret to film the short documentary *Students* (1973), about the student underground, which got his films banned by the junta. He supported himself abroad by working on and also acting in films for friends, including Rossellini's *Anno Uno*, Fellini's *City of Women*, Francesco Rosi's *Christ Stopped at Eboli* and the Taviani Brothers' *Allonsanfàn*.

Returning from exile in the 1980s, he began work on a series of drastically low-budget art house gems such as *Balamos* (1982), *Danilo Treles* (1985) and *A Heron for Germany* (1987). As Stavros Kaplanidis' wonderful documentary about him, *Stavros Tornes: The Poor Hunter of the South* (1994), showed, Tornes' films were sometimes put together on his kitchen table with a budget found in the lining of his jacket or cadged from his many doting friends. While his production budgets were non-existent, Tornes may one day be regarded as a poet-philosopher of Greek cinema equal and perhaps, considering his *arte povera* philosophy, even superior to Angelopoulos.

Athenian Theatre: a Long Intermission

The history of drama in Athens parallels that of its architecture: a brilliant opening act in theatres built by Pericles, no less, for the inventors of theatre, followed by a Beckettian intermission of two thousand years, and then, in the late nineteenth century, a sudden reappearance of the cast on stage, when even Robert Wilson or Jan Fabre might have expected the audience to have long ago left the auditorium. There had been earlier theatre in Greece, such as sixteenth-century drama in Crete (including work by the poet Vitsentzos Kornaros), and Italian-influenced drama and light opera in the Ionians during Venetian rule, as well as the travelling *karagiozis* shadow theatres. But modern Greek theatre was an invention of Athens in the nineteenth century—though it could be said that many of these latter-day satires and tragedies were reviving the traditions of the classical masters.

Although a small theatre was operating on the city limits in 1840, we might date the official birth of modern Greek theatre to 1880, when King George I declared that the nation should have a National Theatre, and the expatriate businessman Efstratios Rallis donated £100,000 (worth perhaps as much as five million today, according to one index) to build it. The theatre opened in 1900, and by 1903 had its first controversy, when a version of Aeschylus' *Oresteia* in demotic Greek sparked riots by pro-*katharevousa* students that left one dead and ten injured. The theatre continued staging otherwise uncontroversial classical and modern productions until 1908, when it went dark. Apart from occasionally hosting visiting companies from abroad, the theatre remained shuttered until 1932, when it re-opened with new productions of Aeschylus' *Agamemnon* and a contemporary drama by the novelist Grigorios Xenopoulos. In 1938 it staged the first modern production in the open air theatre at Epidaurus, a performance of Sophocles' *Elektra*, and later established the Epidaurus Festival in 1954. Its artistic director Kostis Bastias also imported productions from abroad, in 1938 from London's Old Vic and Dublin's Gate theatres, a tradition that continues today.

The following year the first Greek National Opera company was established at the National Theatre, with a production of Strauss' *Die*

Fledermaus, and its staging of Puccini's *Tosca* in 1942 featured the debut performance by an as-yet unknown New York-born Greek singer, Maria Callas. (Callas, then nineteen, had returned to Athens from New York when her parents separated, and studied and performed in the city until leaving for Italy, and legend, less than three years later.)

Callas' debut took place during troubled times in Athens, at the depths of the Nazi-era famine, but clearly the artistic life of the city continued regardless, for the same year the director Karolos Koun formed his legendary Theatro Technis (Art Theatre, and probable model for the modern London theatre foundation of the same name). Koun became famous for avant-garde productions of the classics, but also for introducing contemporary theatre to Greek audiences, importing works by Anouilh, Brecht, Lorca, O'Neill, Pirandello and Tennessee Williams (Melina Mercouri's first major success was as Blanche DuBois in Koun's National Theatre production of *A Streetcar Named Desire*, a production also featuring some of the earliest music by someone else we are about to encounter, Manos Hadjidakis).

Koun balanced often heretical readings of the classics, such as Aristophanes' *The Birds*, and combative contemporary works by the likes of Genet and Ionesco. He set the tone for a modern Greek theatre that could both reinvent the classics (even if it was sometimes astride a motorcycle) and also import the European avant-garde, such as his 1952 National Theatre production of Pirandello's *Henry IV*, in which the playwright recasts Shakespeare's original digression into the ravings of a delusional actor in 1920s Italy.

This climate also bred new writers who similarly fed off both the old and the new, most famously the playwright and novelist Iakovos Kambanellis, whose earliest plays were produced at the National Theatre and by Koun at his Theatro Technis. Kambanellis, a survivor of the Mauthausen concentration camp who later wrote the *Mauthausen Cantata* (1965) with Mikis Theodorakis, frequently hijacked figures from ancient myth and drama and transported them into the modern day: in his later *A Comedy* (1995), Persephone and Pluto are among the shareholders in a leisure corporation that wants to remodel Hades as a tourism resort to rival Mykonos. Kambanellis also addressed contemporary social realism, particularly in his early *Courtyard of Miracles* (1957), set in an Athens tenement, which also saw contemporary Greek theatre being exported abroad, with a production in London in 1961. His most famous work was, however, for the cinema: he co-wrote Cacoyannis' *Stella*, and Nikos Koundouros' abovementioned *O Drakos*.

The period of the late 1950s and early 1960s saw a number of similar experimental theatre groups sprouting in Athens, embracing concepts such as the Theatre of the Absurd, importing playwrights such as Albee, Beckett and Pinter, and also nurturing homegrown talent such as Loula Anagnostaki, whose plays such as *Victory* (1978) explore a particularly Greek brand of Pinteresque domestic menace. The period also saw the earliest works by Kostas Mourselas, whose later quintet of short plays *This One ... and That One* (1975), a Beckettian series about two educated tramps discussing the meaning of life, was inevitably banned by the Colonels' culture police.

The Colonels, of course, put paid to any such subversion in the arts in general, and that applied to Aeschylus, Socrates and Sophocles as much as it did to Samuel Beckett and The Beatles. If anything, however, this propelled writers into finding new ways to get their work past the censor's blue pencil, and at least fifty new plays were produced in Athens during the years 1970 to 1974. The Colonels did manage to re-stage Aeschylus' *Oresteia* as a propaganda piece; conversely, artists were fleeing the country, being jailed or exiled internally, or, in the case of Melina Mercouri, having their citizenship revoked while working abroad.

The sombre mood that delivered a conservative government after the fall of the Colonels saw a fading of the pre-junta radicalism, as playwrights either sought new directions in post-modernism or structuralism, such as Yorgos Dialegmenos in *Mother, Mom, Mama* (1980) and Dimitris Kehaidis and Eleni Haviara in *Laurels and Oleanders* (1988), or transgressive comedy, such as Yorgos Maniotis' *The Pit* (1981). Others migrated into cinema, most notably Stratis Karras, nowadays better known as a collaborator with Theo Angelopoulos, and Pavlos Matesis, likewise better known now for his bestselling novel *The Daughter* (2002), which has been widely touted as an imminent film from the controversial Serbian director Emir Kusturica.

The radicalism persists, however, not least in smaller and experimental venues such as Bios, where the theatre programming recalls London's ICA at its innovative prime, and also in the smaller auditoriums at the Cacoyannis Foundation, National Theatre and more modest spaces around the city. It can also produce social comment in the tradition of Kambanellis: the AbOvo theatre company's wild satire of contemporary Greek politics, *Mama Ellada* (2008), became a surprise smash hit and even spawned a sequel. The radicalism can also surface in the strangest places, the opening ceremony of the 2004 Olympics being the most notable example. Many people (including *Time* magazine and *The Times* newspaper journalists who declared it a "triumph") among the estimated 127 million global television audience probably mistook the hour-long opening extravaganza as some Cirque du Soleil-type spectacle, which is perhaps a mark of how the mainstream can absorb the avant-garde. It was actually the work of Dimitris Papaioannou, a renegade dramatist with origins in Athens' small but lively counter-cultural underground whose ambitions and career trajectory could very possibly see him taking a curtain call at Bayreuth before long.

Born in Athens in 1964, Papaioannou studied with the painter Yannis Tsarouchis while still in his teens, displaying a precocious talent that won him entry into the School of Art, where he studied under the expressionist and Critical Realist painter Dimitris Mytaras. Papaioannou's first art works were illustrations and comic designs in the alternative Athens press in the 1980s, particularly the media springing up to give a voice to the city's nascent gay culture. He designed for theatre and dance groups while at the Art School, and studied dance and performance in the USA with Erick Hawkins, a protégé of Martha Graham, and the Butoh-influenced choreographer Maureen Fleming at the legendary La MaMa Experimental Theatre Club in Manhattan.

Returning to Athens in 1986, he founded his own dance group, Edafos ("ground"), producing stark, minimal and startling move-

ment pieces that bring to mind the punishing body workouts of
Édouard Lock's La La La Human Steps, Pina Bausch's Tanztheater
Wuppertal and others. This only pointed in one direction, and by
1989 he was in Germany assisting Robert Wilson on *The Black Rider*,
Wilson's typically enigmatic collaboration with Tom Waits and
William Burroughs. (Perhaps tellingly, both Bausch and Wilson are,
or in the case of Bausch, who died in 2009, were, regular visitors to
Athens.) Papaioannou also assisted Wilson on his later experimental dramatization of Virginia Woolf's *Orlando*. Returning to Athens
again, he started winning awards at home and abroad for his own
multimedia performance pieces, including *The Last Song of Richard
Strauss* (1990), which represented Greece at the Seville Expo 92, and
found a fan in the then Minister of Culture, Melina Mercouri, who
helped find government support for Papaioannou's work. By the
1990s the *New York Times* was already dispatching stringers to review
him in Lisbon, Lyon and elsewhere, particularly following the international success of his dance work *Medea* (1993), in which performers negotiated a waterlogged set dominated by very Wilson-like
angular sets and lighting techniques. (It has since acquired a first-
night-of-*Einstein-on-the-Beach*-moment aura among Athens
theatre-goers.) He also turned his hand to operas, both modern (with
composer Thanos Mikroutsikos) and classical (Bellini's *La
Sonnambula*), in addition to choreography for Michael Cacoyannis,
productions at the National Theatre and a version of Cherubini's
Medea. In 2001 Papaioannou became a daring appointment as
Artistic Director for the planned 2004 Olympics celebrations.

The Opening ceremonies of the Olympics are said to have come
in under the estimated budget of thirty-three million euros (of an
approximate nine billion post-hangover Olympics budget), and apart
from some hi-tech effects were probably cheaper to produce than
the Pink Floyd stage show the man from *The Times* compared them
to. Borrowing a few tricks from Robert Wilson's book of minimal-
ist staging, Papaioannou and a production team of 435 people de-
ployed an estimated 2482 volunteers across an indoor sea in a tableau
vivant of Greek history, with mythical creatures, legendary figures
(including a topless Minoan princess whose breasts had to be pixil-

lated for timid US TV viewers), living Parthenon friezes and Byzantine icons, a gigantic Cycladic figurine head that opened to reveal a man scrambling over a Pythagorean cube, laser projections, water sculptures, and that young boy aboard that very Wilson-like giant paper boat. Wilson himself would have killed for that sort of budget and logistics (his *the CIVIL warS*, planned for the opening of the 1984 Summer Olympics in Los Angeles, fell apart when funding failed to materialize), but afterwards Papaioannou returned to more modest projects, such as *2* (2006), the updated *Medea²* (2008), and the sea-borne *HEAVEN LIVE AB2* at Palaio Faliro beach for the 2009 Athens Biennale, some of which were seen by a hundred thousand people. He is edging ever closer to that curtain-call at Bayreuth, where Greek theatre may finally deliver a long-overdue black eye to Otto's Bavarocracy, and by a man history may come to regard as a genius.

7

The Sound of the City
Music Old and Modern

As in literature and the visual arts, music in Greece was cut off from most strands of European culture prior to the eighteenth century. Beyond a rich heritage of devotional music and myriad regional folk forms, what Greek classical music existed had either been imported from, or was imitative of, northern European styles, particularly the traditions introduced by Italian occupiers in the Ionian Islands—most famously in the shape of the Corfiot Nikolaos Mantzaros, composer of the music for Dionysios Solomos' national anthem, "Hymn to Liberty". The popularity of Italian *bel canto* light opera also influenced local song forms, notably the *arekia* and *kantathes* traditions of Zakynthos and elsewhere. The late nineteenth and early twentieth centuries saw indigenous composers emerging, but again largely influenced from abroad. They included Spyridon Samaras, who composed the music to Palamas' Olympic Anthem and, as an expatriate in Italy, wrote many operas influenced by his teachers at the Paris Conservatoire, among them Delibes, Gounod and Massenet. We should also mention Aristotelis Koundouroff, who studied in Moscow and would be compared to both Prokofiev and Scriabin; Dimitri Mitropoulos, better known in his adopted USA as a conductor, for the New York Philharmonic, the Met and Boston Symphony; and Marios Varvoglis, a contemporary of Ravel and Varèse. Although trained in Paris, Varvoglis taught at the Athens Conservatory from the 1920s onwards, and his left-leaning politics led him into confrontations with the government—to the extent that he was held in a British concentration camp after the Second World War.

Three Great Composers
Varvoglis' experiences set a template for the troubled interactions

between the three great Greek composers of the twentieth century and the state: Manos Hadjidakis, Mikis Theodorakis and Iannis Xenakis. Of the three, Theodorakis is the most famous, with a vast canon to his name and an unequalled renown as a politician and human rights activist. Iannis Xenakis was born in Romania but raised in Greece, educated in Athens and bloodied on its streets during both wars. Smuggled into exile in Paris, he became the supreme Greek modernist composer of his generation, and the only Greek to stand alongside the likes of Berio, Boulez, Ligeti and Stockhausen in the post-war European avant-garde.

If any of the three can be said to have had a lasting effect on Greek music and culture, however, it has to be Hadjidakis. I write "has to" not out of reluctance, but because Hadjidakis was a mainstream, populist composer (perhaps comparable, in his light song cycles—the style was known as *entekno*, or "art song"—to Samuel Barber or Ned Rorem) who acted as a catalyst in various ways, not least encouraging the young Xenakis, but also telling the Greeks themselves to pay attention to the music that was being played in their neighbourhood *kafeneia*. His impact can be seen in the popular embrace of *rebetiko*, formerly a rebel, underground music, and also in his influence on *laika*, popular song, from the 1960s *Nea Kyma* (New Wave) of Greek chart pop to its more unlikely current manifestations, including the twenty-first century recordings of electronica darlings Stereo Nova (Greece's answer to Orbital) and Panos Kyveleas' one-man experimental group Biomass, which mixes sampled Cretan lyre and Eastern folk forms with dub reggae and electronics. What Hadjidakis might have made of this is anyone's guess, although given his spirit of adventure he would probably have approved.

Hadjidakis was born in Xanthi, a city in the tobacco-growing region east of Thessaloniki, but raised in Athens. The early death of his father forced the teenage Hadjidakis to work as a stevedore in Piraeus, a line worker at the Fix beer brewery, a hospital nursing assistant, and elsewhere. He also studied music, prior to entering the Greek National Music School in Athens, and became friends with the poet Nikos Gatsos, who would be a life-long collaborator.

Hadjidakis studied under the classical composer Menelaos Pallandios, and made his first public steps with music for Karolos Koun's radical Theatro Technis theatre group, where he met another lifelong friend and collaborator, Melina Mercouri. As well as writing the music for the production of *Streetcar* in which Mercouri played Blanche DuBois, Hadjidakis also composed for productions of O'Neill's *Mourning Becomes Electra*, Lorca's *Blood Wedding* and Miller's *Death of a Salesman*. He also began writing for the cinema, including Cacoyannis' *Stella* and Kazan's *America, America*, but it was *Never on Sunday* (1960) and the Oscar for its title song that made his name—and his fortune.

This was an incredibly busy period in Hadjidakis' career, writing for ballet, film, opera and theatre. The popularity of "Never on Sunday" led to his work being recorded by Harry Belafonte, Nat "King" Cole, Brenda Lee, Johnny Mathis and Nana Mouskouri, with whom he also developed a lifelong friendship and collaboration. He also found time to launch the Competition for Avant-Garde Composers at the Athens Technological Organization, whose first winner, in 1962, was the virtually unknown Xenakis, and the following year he founded the Athens Experimental Orchestra, expressly to showcase contemporary Greek composers. He would also found his own Polytropon café-theatre in Athens, initiating the arts journal *Tetarto* and establishing the record label Sirius to promote young Greek musicians (it was still signing young groups, such as the now-defunct The Earthbound, in the 2000s). He accepted roles in various government organizations, too: as director of the State Opera, then the State Orchestra, and also Greek National Radio's Third Programme.

Despite these establishment connections, Hadjidakis was outspoken on many liberal-left issues throughout his career (unabashedly homosexual, he joined other celebrities at the head of Athens' first ever gay pride march in 1977), even if—like Theodorakis after him—he also dallied with Nea Demokratia during the period of widespread disillusion with Andreas Papandreou's PASOK.

Perhaps his most memorable performance, however, was at Karolos Koun's Theatro Technis in 1949, when Hadjidakis delivered his now-legendary lecture on *rebetiko*. Despite British commander Ronald Scobie's mischievous use of *rebetiko* as a propaganda device in the early days of the Civil War, it remained a controversial musical form, associated with a shadowy demi-monde of alcohol, drugs, crime and immorality. Hadjidakis' lecture tracked it back to origins in Byzantine times, dared his audience to mock when he compared it to Beethoven, but argued, above all, that *rebetiko* was the one profoundly Greek art form above any other. Half a century on, Hadjidakis' arguments are commonplace, but at the time they were scandalous. While later governments would suppress the music, Hadjidakis almost single-handedly ushered *rebetiko* into the academy, including, eventually, the big one built by Theophil Hansen on Panepistimiou Street. Musician and writer Gail Holst's book *Road to Rembetika* remains the key text on the history of this music, although Elias Petropoulos' hard-to-find underground classic, *Rebetika: Songs from the Greek Underworld* offers a first-hand account of the milieu from an author who appalled Greek society by embracing its underclasses.

Born the same year as Hadjidakis, on the island of Chios, Mikis Theodorakis continues to compose and campaign to this day, and can also thank one single tune, his "Zorba's Dance" from Cacoyannis' *Zorba the Greek*, for early international fame, although the theme was originally composed by the Cretan composer Giorgis Koutsourelis, as "Armenohorianos Syrtos". (A bizarre internet legend claims it later became a favourite of Peru's terrorist Sendero Luminoso leader Abimael Guzmán, who may or may not be the bearded individual seen dancing to it on a popular YouTube clip.)

Theodorakis' curriculum vitae is even longer than Hadjidakis', and in 2010 was rather sweetly topped, after his eighty-fifth birthday celebrations, by a dance floor remix of his hits by the cult Ibiza DJ Francesco Diaz, including a trip-hop reading of the Zorba theme co-produced by Theodorakis himself.

Theodorakis was largely self-taught, beginning to write songs in his childhood, but took formal music lessons in his teens. Even before moving to Athens in 1943, aged eighteen, he had been jailed for left wing activities in Tripolis, and credits fellow inmates with introducing him to Marxism, prompting him to join the KKE. His further education was disrupted by the Second World War, and on arriving to study at the Athens Conservatoire he became a member of EPON, the United Panhellenic Organization of Youth, and joined a reserve unit of ELAS, the Greek People's Liberation Army, the following year. Theodorakis was involved in the anti-British demonstrations at the start of the Civil War, waking up after one fracas on a mortuary slab having been found unconscious with a fractured skull and presumed dead. In 1947 he was arrested and jailed on the island of Ikaria before being sent for "re-education" at the concentration camp on Makronisi, along with an estimated thirty thousand others. During his time on Makronisi, Theodorakis was tortured numerous times and buried alive twice, experiences that would inform his work up to the present day. Incredibly, after the Civil War was over, Theodorakis was still required to complete military service, during which time his politics earned him further, near-fatal, beatings. He graduated summa cum laude from the Conservatoire in 1950, but only extricated himself from the military in 1952, when he became a music critic for the newspaper *Avghi* and began composing for ballet, theatre and film. He studied with Messiaen in Paris, premiered his "Sonatina for Piano" there in 1955, and in 1956 wrote his first major film soundtrack, for Powell and Pressburger's *Ill Met by Moonlight*.

He returned to Greece in 1960, despite receiving a death threat warning him against ever stepping on to Greek soil again (he replied by publishing the date and time of his flight to Athens). Settled, he embarked on a dual career as composer and perennial thorn in the side of governments of any shade. The year 1964 was particularly fruitful, with the release of both *Zorba the Greek* and the completion of his early masterpiece, *Axion Esti*, an oratorio setting of Odysseus Elytis' epic poem. On 21 April 1967, the day of the Colonels' coup, Theodorakis went into hiding, and three weeks later the regime released its first list of banned materials, including "Army Order No. 13" forbidding the reproduction or performance of the music of Theodorakis. In July he was arrested, put in a variety of prisons, and finally placed under house arrest at his holiday home in Vrachati, near Corinth, where he became an international *cause célèbre*, with figures such as Leonard Bernstein and Dmitri Shostakovich campaigning on his behalf. Taken to a military prison suffering from recurrent tuberculosis in 1970, he was released as part of an amnesty and moved, still sick, to Paris, where he promptly launched a campaign against the regime and began a series of world tours to publicize his "declaration of war" against the Colonels. The exiled Theodorakis became the singular symbol of the Greek resistance.

He flew back to Athens the day after the Colonels fell, to a hero's welcome at the airport, and resumed that dual career as composer and activist. His first symphony of 1953 would be followed by six more, along with numerous oratorios and choral works, such as the *Mauthausen* oratorio with Iakovos Kambanellis, operas and theatre works, film scores and ballet pieces, as well as collections of often political songs, most recently the CD releases *Eighteen Little Songs for the Bitter Homeland* and *The Political Agenda*. His politics have remained staunchly humanitarian, even if his party allegiances have traversed the spectrum from the KKE, for whom he stood, unsuccessfully, in the 1960s; via PASOK, which saw him briefly accept a ministerial role in the 1980s; to Nea Demokratia, when he joined the intellectuals' exodus from Andreas Papandreou's PASOK. As recently as 2010, he was skirmishing in public with George Papandreou over the latter's attempts to "blackmail" the public into supporting PASOK in the November 2010 elections, making headlines by saying that if a centre-right party had attempted what Papandreou was attempting, the left would have "set Greece on fire".

His music has always been bound to his politics, which some might say has hampered his art. But when he has succeeded, in works such as *Axion Esti* and *Mauthausen*, he has attained his goal of a "metasymphonic" music that goes beyond genre and narrative to combine classical with folk forms in pieces that stand alongside epochal works such as Britten's *War Requiem* and Tippett's *A Child of Our Time*.

Iannis Xenakis chose a career path that rendered the idea of popularity irrelevant, even though some of his works drew hundreds of thousands, comparable to the crowds who flocked to Dimitris

Papaioannou's recent extravaganzas. In his pursuit of music using game theory and random processes, he was probably the most intensely cerebral of those post-war European avant-gardists. He never became a media celebrity in the manner of John Cage or Karlheinz Stockhausen—although there are signs of a revival of interest in his work, not least in the USA, where a large Xenakis festival dominated the summer of 2010 in New York and elsewhere.

When Xenakis was ten his family returned to Greece from Romania following the death of his mother, and he was sent to an international school on Spetses, where he excelled at maths, literature and music. Maths took him in the direction of architecture (he would later become a fractious assistant to Le Corbusier), which he studied at the Athens Polytechnic. He also embarked on a parallel study of music with Koundouroff, even though his final thesis at the Polytechnic was a paper on the wonders of reinforced concrete. He too found his studies disrupted by the Second World War, and after a flirtation with a far-right resistance group Xenakis joined EAM, the KKE-led National Liberation Front, and was arrested and jailed several times during street battles with the Nazis. When the British replaced the Nazis on the streets of Athens, Xenakis joined the student battalion of ELAS, becoming commander of the Lord Byron Unit until felled by a mortar during a street skirmish with British tanks. With serious facial injuries and an eye knocked out, Xenakis was left for dead, but his father found him and took him to hospital. He recovered sufficiently to complete his studies, and also to continue with his activism, which led to several arrests and finally imprisonment. His father managed to procure a false passport and smuggled Xenakis out of the country, for which both his father and brother were jailed, while Xenakis was sentenced to death in absentia.

Xenakis ended up in Paris, where his qualifications won him a job as an engineer with Le Corbusier. He also attempted to continue his music studies. A friend recommended him to Olivier Messiaen, who invited him to attend his classes, alongside a young German composer, Karlheinz Stockhausen. While Stockhausen worked towards pieces such as *Kontra-Punkte* and *Kreuzspiele*, Xenakis applied Le Corbusier's ideas of maths combined with Einstein's theories about time to an evocation of the sounds of warfare in his first major work, *Meta-staseis* (1953), for 61-piece orchestra, an alarming vision of the future of music which still makes the early Stockhausen seem tame in comparison. *Meta-staseis* also employed systems borrowed from the Fibonacci series, a concept Xenakis later applied to architectural projects, such as his pointily space-age Philips Pavilion at Expo 58 in Brussels. Xenakis would go on to apply game and set theories to solo and group percussion works (anyone who thinks Steve Reich's *Drumming* is the last word in percussion music should strap themselves in for an exhilarating ride through Xenakis' "Psappha" or *Pleiades*), and particularly in acoustic and electronic pieces using his UPIC computer system, an early form of sequencer which later found great favour with a younger generation, not least British ambient composer Aphex Twin.

In 1968 Xenakis combined architecture and music with his first "Polytope", a term from geometry for any multi-sided form and alluding to the multi-media aspect of these music/sculpture/light performance pieces. Xenakis applied the polytope idea to numerous specific sites, starting with Montreal for Expo 67, a later site-specific work at Mycenae, and most famously, the *Polytope de Cluny*, in 1972, when an estimated 200,000 people visited Xenakis' laser, light and sound installation at the Roman baths in the Musée de Cluny in Paris. By this time Xenakis was a star of the international new music circuit, lionized by festivals and state orchestras, garlanded with awards from around the world, and more or less able to write his own specification (and cheque) for any commission.

Although he acquired French citizenship, he was back in Athens in the 1960s, no longer under sentence of death, and after the fall of the Colonels he was the subject of a "Xenakis Week" at the 1975 Athens Festival. His "A Héléne", a choral work from Euripides' *Helen of Troy*, was premiered at Epidaurus in 1977, and the *Polytope de Mycenae* was staged there in 1978. Later orchestral and operatic works would also borrow from Greek literature and myth, but in addition to influences from other cultures, particularly the Far East, such as the startling earlier "Habiki Hana Ma" for Expo 70 in Osaka, written for orchestra, eight hundred loud speakers and a computerized sound system.

Unlike figures such as Cage and Stockhausen, whose influence on successive generations is well known, Xenakis' legacy to younger musicians, from Germany's Can to the USA's DJ Spooky, has yet to be fully teased out. There has been no Greek composer of Xenakis' stature for half a century, although there are sounds in the back streets of Athens that suggest his influence is still active a decade after his death. His influence can most immediately be found in young classical composers such as Dionysis Boukouvalas, an aficionado of minimalists such as Wim Mertens as well as the electroacoustic mafia; Kyriakos Sfetsas, who actually worked with Xenakis as well as Luigi Nono and Henri Dutilleux; Panayiotis Kokoras, president of the Hellenic Electroacoustic Composers Association and Lefteris Papadimitriou, possibly Athens' (and, occasionally, Huddersfield's) very own maximalist in the manner of Steve Martland or Glenn Branca. Greece bristles with small contemporary ensembles, but special note should be made of the Athens Arts Ensemble, who cite Xenakis alongside influences including The Cure, Massive Attack and Kraftwerk, and in 2009 premiered a work inspired by the police killing of fifteen-year-old student Alexis Grigoropoulos on the streets of Exarheia in 2008.

From the Summer of Love to Post-Punk Haikus

Greece's "rock'n'roll moment" ended almost as soon as it began: 1967, the "summer of love" that saw the release of *Sergeant Pepper* and *Magical Mystery Tour*, The Rolling Stones' *Their Satanic Majesties Request*, Hendrix's *Are You Experienced?*, debuts from The Doors, Pink Floyd, The Velvet Underground and many more, saw tanks on the streets of Athens and elsewhere when on 21 April the Colonels staged their coup. While some joined the writers and filmmakers in exile, others, such as Dionysis Savvopoulos, stayed to kick up a fuss, even if that fuss was influenced largely by Bob Dylan and Frank Zappa. Greece's most famous band of the era, Aphrodite's Child, who would go on to sell more than twenty million albums, had already decamped to London for career reasons, and their five years together, before leading members Demis Roussos and Vangelis Papathanassiou left to pursue solo careers, were spent in England, France and Italy. By the time of their most famous release, the 1972 album *666*, the group had already disbanded.

Dionysis Savvopoulos was jailed for his political activism in 1967, and like counterparts from the era had to develop strategies to get around the censors. He has retained his political edge to this day, when he continues to perform and record, and when he has been adopted as a figurehead by younger generations of rock, new wave and post-punk musicians. It is tempting to say that while they (indeed *because* they) were deprived of it, Greeks took to rock music like no other European culture, even if much of it, up to and including much latterday Greek rock, is imitative of British and North American styles. It is noteworthy, however, that the great majority of Greek bands insist on singing in their own language, rather than the unhappy mid-Atlantic English of many northern European groups.

While a native audience will find a reason to explain Greek-language heavy metal, the rest of the world may wonder at the need for another Judas Priest or Iron Maiden in a different language. We could say the same about much Greek punk, however admirable the indie ethics, and it is only with the experimentation that followed punk that we see bands such as Stereo Nova finding a uniquely new Greek voice in a mix of modern and traditional forms.

There are even more interesting composers working in the gap between contemporary music and whatever we can call post-punk music today. Chief among these is Coti K, born Constantino Luca Rolando Kiriakos to Greek parents in Milan in 1966, but an Athenian since the age of six and a mainstay of the Athens music scene since the 1980s. He first came to international notice in the 1990s as producer for, among others, the cult San Francisco art-punk group Tuxedomoon (whose Blaine Reininger, also a sometime Coti K collaborator, has been based in Athens for over a decade as a musician and actor) on albums such as *Cabin in the Sky*, *Bardo Hotel* and *Vapour Trails*. He is better known at home as the "fourth" member of local legends Stereo Nova. Typical of the inter-connectedness of many Athens arts figures, Coti K has also provided the music to films by Angelos Frantzis (both *A Dog's Dream* and *In the Woods*), theatre works by *Dogtooth* director Yorgos Lanthimos, and some of the mixed-media spectacles of Dimitris Papaioannou (*Nowhere* and *Medea²*).

More recently, Coti K has racked up eight solo albums, the latest being *Dunung* and *Onda*, dark electronic soundscapes that hark back to Xenakis but also to US minimalists such as LaMonte Young. His most recent project is the noise supergroup Mohammad, co-founded with the second of our suspects, Athenian cellist Nikos Veliotis, locally notorious for a work that might have borrowed from the Fluxus Group—destroying a cello—recording the event and releasing just one hundred copies of the CD, *Cello Powder*, with a jar of dust from the pulverized instrument as a keepsake. Veliotis has also recorded with pianist John Tilbury, the great interpreter of Morton Feldman's works, and Fred van Hove, the Dutch pianist noted for his work on Peter Brotzmann's legendary free jazz recording, *Machine Gun*. We should also include Bill Kouligas, whose one-man noise-generating group Family Battle Snake has supported Sonic Youth on tour and had to be conceived in the shadow of Xenakis' ear-splitting *Mycenae-Alpha*.

Coti K's former colleagues Stereo Nova provide us with a handy bridge to the Athenian pop mainstream. Formed at the beginning of the 1990s, this electronica trio swiftly became the key figures in Greece's dance underground, cleverly adapting house and techno to sampled or forged *rebetiko* instrumentation, stealing so astutely from Kraftwerk that some pieces amount to an uncollected Christmas present to Kraftwerk's lawyers. Yet, an abiding theme in good contemporary Greek music of any form, they are also aware of their heritage, hence those sampled baglamas and lyres and their enticing of 1960s Nea Kyma pop icon Popi Asteriadi (Greece's answer to Pet Clark, or perhaps Mireille Mathieu) to sing with them on *Ofelimo Fortio*, their collaboration with modern *laika* pop idol Stamatis Kraounakis. Stereo Nova broke up in 1999, reforming briefly in 2008 for a swan-song party organized by *Lifo*, Athens' version of *Village Voice*. The two key members, K.Bhta and Mikaël Delta, have since pursued solo careers, the former following a more avant-garde path and contributing music to Pappaioannou's Olympic spectacles in 2004. Delta has mined a more dance-oriented groove, with eight solo albums to date and film projects including the soundtrack to Panos Koutras' *Real Life*.

Stereo Nova have presided over an entire younger generation of adventurous Athenian and Greek pop acts, such as Spyweirdos, Qebo, One Hour Before the Trip, DJ Nikko Patrelakis and many others, often to be found on labels such as Triple Bath and AntiFrost, perhaps the Greek equivalents of labels such as Mute or Warp. They and their compatriots can also be heard live at festivals such as Synch, which is where this writer stumbled across the furious electro-dub-*rebetiko* of Biomass, and also the lyrical Cretan folk melded with Durutti Column-like keyboard loops of Tasman.

Athens is also host to various other music festivals, most famously the summertime Rockwave, the majority more mainstream than Synch. Like most continental European countries, Greece tolerates its indigenous heavy metal culture, just as it does reggae and post-punk too. (You want Radiohead? Try the now-defunct but cultish Raining Pleasure. Or perhaps New Order? Consider the Athenian combo Film. The list grows daily.) It also has a surprisingly large home-grown hip-hop culture, sung in Greek, best found in its dedicated section of Public, the Megastore-style chain often found in university towns. Greek-language hip-hop, in a country where *rebetiko* out-bad-mouthed Niggaz With Attitude nearly a century ago, might prove a post-modern linguistic detour too recondite for some.

What is missing here, of course, is *rebetiko* itself, but its rich and storied background has an ample history well recorded elsewhere, in English as well as Greek. Less recorded, perhaps, is what newer Greek singers and songwriters are minting from tradition, not least performers such as Savina Yannatou and Lena Platonos, who are refining the influences of elders such as the iconic Maria Farantouri. Farantouri, dubbed "the Joan Baez of the Mediterranean" by *Le Monde*, was a longtime friend and collaborator of Hadjidakis, acted as Theodorakis' "voice" in Greece during his exile and a performer who draws vast crowds at home and in concert halls and opera houses from New York to Moscow. Yannatou, with her group

Primavera en Salonico, has plugged into a whole network of Mediterranean musical forms that would require an entire book or more to untangle. Platonos, hailed as the natural spiritual heir to both Hadjidakis and Farantouri, leans more towards the avant-garde, which is a shameless excuse for a namecheck for my friend, the opera-trained vocal terrorist Diamanda Galás, American born and bred, but an Athenian to her bones. No life is complete without a night spent cowering behind the sofa from her voice. (Diamanda has, perhaps unsurprisingly, also worked with Xenakis...)

Yannatou has recorded a number of albums for the German jazz/contemporary label ECM, where she shares catalogue space with the Athenian pianist Vassilis Tsabropoulos, probably the most commendable individual one can dredge from what is at best a sorry excuse for a Greek jazz culture. Tsabropoulos is a lovely player, echoing Keith Jarrett as well as the keyboard works of Satie and Chopin (who, along with Rachmaninov and Prokofiev, is a key figure in his classical repertoire), and can be heard with jazz luminaries Arild Andersen and John Marshall on the ECM recording *The Promise*. The only wild surmise I can make on the lack of a credible jazz scene in either Athens or Greece as a whole is that the cultural forces that produced jazz elsewhere found their focus here in *rebetiko* and other folk forms. Athens' sole jazz club, the Half-Note, has a splendid policy of programming dance music from South America to Africa to the Balkans, but somehow forgets to programme *jazz*.

If there is a work from the contemporary Athens music scene that any adventurous listener should hunt down, it is the small masterpiece by Sigmatropic, *Sixteen Haiku and Other Stories*, which spans millennia of Greek culture and also most of the world's musics. Sigmatropic is the project of one man, composer Akis Boyatzis, working largely at home on a PC. He performs occasionally with a Greek line-up of Sigmatropic, and for *Sixteen Haiku* was joined by a border-hopping coterie of long-distance collaborators, including Robert Wyatt, Laetitia Sadier from Stereolab, James Sclavunos of The Bad Seeds, Carla Torgersen of The Walkabouts, Mark Eitzel from American Music Club and Lee Ranaldo of Sonic Youth. *Sixteen Haiku* takes its title and texts from a little-known work by

George Seferis, a series of haiku written almost as an exercise in style while Seferis was working on his translation of T. S. Eliot's "The Waste Land" in London. Seferis' often sea-bound haiku stretch back to the myth of Persephone and up to contemporary geopolitics. Boyatzis' influences extend to teen memories of The Residents and Pere Ubu, folk-rock *à la* Fairport Convention, Canterbury eccentrics such as Caravan and the Hatfields, up to the spikier parts of post-punk, from Sonic Youth to the likes of Yeah Yeah Yeahs, as well as an ocean of electronica sound. The result is a "concept album" that resembles a mad, inspired, chamber opera as it might be fashioned by Van Dyke Parks or Carla Bley in her *Escalator Over the Hill* days. (We should also probably invoke Syd Barrett and Nick Drake, as well as Randy Newman and Stan Ridgway.) I am loath to load it with comparisons to *Pet Sounds* or *Sergeant Pepper* for fear of ageing it, but the creative accomplishment deserves the comparison. *Sixteen Haiku* is a work of twenty-first century Greek genius. To date, however, this most international of modern Greek masterpieces is largely unknown in the city and country that produced it.

8 | Leisure and Pleasure
Popular Culture and Pastimes

ven if "true" Athenians "never" visit the Acropolis, between the Parthenon and the privacy of the Athenian home there is still an entire city where the visitor can play as the Athenians play. (And if the early crowds who pressed into the new Acropolis Museum after it opened in June 2009 are any gauge, plenty of "true" Athenians do want to visit.) Some visitors will find the tourist circuit more than enough to explore on a visit; others may find their accommodation pitches them into the heart of a neighbourhood culture almost as fascinating as the statuary and architecture the guidebooks say you should not miss.

The Athenian day starts early. Athenians are often at their workplace by eight, but sometimes unavailable between ten and eleven, as they are out for breakfast. Lunch begins at two at the latest, and while the siesta is beginning to blur into all-day opening hours in Athens and other cities, its banks, government offices and other institutions do not open to the public again until the following day and never at weekends. Although smaller and upmarket shops still observe the ten-until-two, five-until-eight (six-until-nine in winter) tradition, many supermarkets and larger businesses are now adopting the seven/eleven timetable.

Evenings start and end late, often beginning in a bar for a drink and *mezedhes*, "little pieces" in the manner of Spanish tapas, followed by a meal and then more, usually abstemious, socializing (public drunkenness is still a rarity in Greece, and typically involves tourists). Like that of its Mediterranean European neighbours, Greek social life still revolves around τα οιχογενεια ("ta oikogenia"), the family, often extended, with all generations staying up late, going out together and even holidaying en masse. The dinner party as conceived in London or New York is regarded as an eccentricity, although

Lunch with a view: The Acropolis from the restaurant of Bernard Tschumi's
hyper-modern Acropolis Museum

family celebrations often migrate to restaurants. Fast food and the shrinking of the extended family are slowly eroding the ritual of the home meal, but Athenians, like the rest of the Greeks, still eat one of the healthiest diets in Europe—even if they are more inclined to smoke afterwards than most other Europeans.

Theatres and cinemas also open late, although the latter, as Greece lacks a film dubbing industry, still show foreign language films with subtitles and the original soundtrack intact. Clubs and music venues rarely come to life before 11pm, although conventional concert halls usually abide by the time it says on the ticket. Despite new laws passed to close clubs in dormitory areas by 3 am, some clubs, music bars and other venues often stay open until dawn or beyond. In high summer, July and August, many clubs and cinemas close down entirely, the former decamping to the Athens coast or the islands, the latter giving way to the many open-air cinemas in the city (a double treat, as they often programme classics and art-house oddities). August is traditionally the month when those who can flee the heat, leaving the city to visitors (who will find this low season in hotel rate terms) and Athenians detained by family or work.

Sporting Athens

Between the nearby mountains and sea you can indulge in water sports, hiking, climbing, cycling and even skiing, but the climate often discourages strenuous outdoor activity. The passive pursuit of sport can be observed in any bar with a working television and ob- servance of the fortunes of Panathinaikos football club approaches a religious fervour. Participatory sports often take a backseat to spec- tator sports, with American basketball and British football also arousing strong passions. (Until the advent of the multi-million lot- teries, Britain's "football pools" gambling system was not only pursued in earnest, but also used as a tool in language schools.) The two main Athens football clubs, Panathinaikos and AEK (Athlitiki Enosis Konstantinoupoleos), currently share the same 75,000-ca- pacity Spiridon Louis Stadium in Maroussi, better known as the 1982 Olympic Stadium (OAKA in abbreviation), built for that year's

European Athletics Championships and one of the main venues for the 2004 Olympics.

Panathinaikos is the oldest Greek football team, formed in 1908, AEK in 1924 by, as its name might suggest, refugees fleeing Constantinople after the pogroms of 1922. The two head Greece's Superleague of the top sixteen city teams, in a season running between August and May during which each team plays a total of thirty games. Both clubs have multilingual websites (and multilingual supporters' clubs), and match dates and reports can be found at their websites and in the sports pages of the English-language press. The clubs sell tickets online, through dedicated offices around the city and tickets are also available at the gate on match days.

The OAKA stadium is part of the 2004 Olympic complex in Maroussi, reached on foot via the Irini or Neratziotissa Metro stations. The Olympic facilities themselves are a continuing scandal in Athens, with most fallen into disuse or administrative dispute, although both the Olympic Aquatic and Tennis Centres are, nominally at least, open to the public—although at prices and a distance that would put them beyond the needs of the casual visitor.

Until December 2010, when the latter title closed due to a slump in revenue directly linked to the financial crisis, the city had two weekly English-language newspapers, *Athens News* and *Athens Plus*, published on Fridays, both with extensive arts and entertainments sections, available at every newspaper *periptero* (street kiosk). Now *Athens News*, published since 1952, dominates an English-language newspaper market of one. It is augmented by three main listings magazines, *Athens Voice, Lifo* and *Athinorama*, all of them in Greek but useful for information if you can negotiate the Greek alphabet. Between them they cover most of what is going on in Athens, and their arts and leisure sections are staffed by younger writers whose opinions are often at some variance from those of the news desk. In the case of the weekly magazines, both *Athens Voice* (which actually adapts the logo of New York's *Village Voice*) and *Lifo* are large-format magazines and comparable to the New York publication before it went A4 and then shifted most of its content to the internet.

Unless the visitor can decode the ever-changing walls of posters that appear throughout the city almost daily, these publications are an essential first-stop for enjoying time off in Athens. The largest cinemas are found in the city centre (often, like the theatres, concealed in arcades) or the more modern ones in mall multiplexes further out from the centre. Art-house cinemas are vanishing from Athens; the art deco wonder of the Rex on Akadimias is now a performance space, although the tiny Titania soldiers on with an eccentric repertory programme, just a few dozen yards into Themistokles Street from Panepistimiou. While the art house cinemas themselves dwindle, arts centres, including Bios, the Cacoyannis Foundation, the Greek Film Archive in Metaxourghio and the Greek Film Center in Trianon Street, also provide more specialist cinematic fare, as do some of the big museums and international cultural institutes, such as the Cervantes and Goethe.

Alfresco Movies and Arts Venues

An Athens institution that the city might claim as unique is its tradition of summertime outdoor cinemas. Their history and culture are roughly equivalent to those of the North American drive-in, although minus the cars: cheap entertainment in an amenable climate without the need for expensive architecture. They are almost as old as Greek cinema itself; the first began in the 1920s, *Cinema Paradiso*-style, with impromptu bring-your-own-chair screenings projected onto the outside wall of a handy bar or café. Most were improvised in open spaces between buildings or in squares or gardens, but as their popularity grew so did their sophistication, with bars, bathrooms, proper flooring and landscape gardening (I owe this history to *Athens News* film critic Despina Pavlaki). They flourished with the post-war movie-going boom and they declined with the advent of television, the VCR and the DVD, although in a city like Athens they remain extremely popular, sociable and neighbourly, untouched by the centralized programming of multiplex chains or television channels, usually with a bar or handy take-out arrangement with a nearby restaurant and cheaper than an evening in with the aircon on. There are still at least sixty summer outdoor cinemas in the city, usually open from July until September, in roofless spaces between buildings, others purpose-built in gardens or squares. Some, such as the Riviera on Valtetsiou Street off Exarheia Square, have an admirable art house programme (but beware: Victor Erice's *Spirit of the Beehive* will be in Spanish with Greek subtitles only). Almost every neighbourhood, including the central ones, will have at least one, but the stars include the Cine Thiseio on Apostolou Pavlou Street, Cine Vox on Exarheia Square, the Ellinis on Kifissias Avenue, the Athinea on Haritos Street in Kolonaki and Cine Psyrri on Sarri Street in Psyrri. The National Museum of Contemporary Art on Vassilis Georgiou has even started throwing the contents of its film archive, including weird and wonderful footage of John Cage and Nam June Paik, onto its exterior walls on summer nights for free.

Music lovers in Athens are well-served at either end of the spectrum, both architecturally and stylistically, but poorly in between. The Megaron Mousikis, also known as the Athens Concert Hall, on Vassilissis Sofias Avenue, is Athens' answer to London's South Bank or New York's Lincoln Center. Opened in 1991 and hailed for its acoustics by a list of notables led by Rostropovich (which puts it ahead of the South Bank venues, at least), it has expanded to four halls of various sizes with an adventurous policy towards homegrown and international music, both old and new, as well as dance and opera. Otherwise, while the Cacoyannis Foundation and newer Onassis Cultural Centre also have music and theatre spaces, and other theatres host occasional music events, there is nowhere in Athens comparable to London venues such as the Academy, Empire or Apollo, or New York equivalents such as the Beacon Theatre, Bowery Ballroom or Mercury Lounge.

The city's longest-running rock venue, Gagarin 205, opened in 1961 and fifty years on is still committed to adventurous music, with a guest book signed over the decades by Iggy Pop & The Stooges, Kraftwerk, OMD, Morrissey, The Residents and others including, more recently, the likes of Kaiser Chiefs and the deeply weird God Speed You! Black Emperor. Slightly younger at a mere twenty-five, An Club on Solomou in Exarheia specializes in the new wave of heavy metal, goth and punk (UK Subs/Vibrators division) but has also found space for idiosyncratic performers such as David Thomas of Pere Ubu, Yo La Tengo, Lydia Lunch and even dub reggae legend Lee "Scratch" Perry. While more mainstream venues such as the Megaron and other theatres also host one-off music events, most are found in dozens of nightclubs, bars and small arts centres such as Bios and About:, an "art/music/poetry/books" space on Miaouli Street in Psirri whose spiritual cousin is probably either London's Riverside Studios or Bristol's Arnolfini Gallery, and where you are most likely to find figures such as Coti K and Nikos Veliotis performing. Bios, on Pireos Street (half a dozen blocks back towards Metaxourghio from Kerameikos Metro station), is more akin to London's ICA or Manhattan's Kitchen or Knitting Factory, a small mixed space for music (recent visitors include ambient legends Autechre and Drexciya spin-off Dopplereffekt), an art gallery, performance space and café/book/music-store/boutique. It is also known for droll performance pieces in which the audience sits inside the venuc watching the production staged on the pavement outside.

Spaces such as About: and Bios exist at the indie/shoestring end of the arts spectrum in a city and country where arts subsidy often comes last in the queue for government handouts, and where private money often either augments or simply replaces state funding. We have already seen this with Dakis Joannou's one-man mini-Heritage of contemporary art at DESTE (which recently opened a satellite gallery, DESTE Hydra, in the old slaughterhouse on the island, more of which later). The two big signature performance spaces in Athens are the Cacoyannis Foundation, some way further down Pireos from Bios, and the recently-opened Onassis Cultural Centre on Syngrou Avenue. The Cacoyannis Foundation, with a 330-seat theatre, 120-seat cinema, black-box performance space, cafés and a rooftop restaurant, opened in March 2010 and its first year featured a rarefied programme mixing Beckett, Garbo, Kurosawa and Pinter, as well as a string of combative indigenous music, theatre and dance events, including an underground car park transformed into a miniature police state and works by the lauded Athens avant-garde dance group MIYA. The Onassis Cultural Centre launched with an inaugural conference on international cultural relations, "The Athens

Dialogues", and has continued with a no less rarefied programme of music, from Family Battle Snake to Savina Yannatou, jazz from Jack DeJohnette and Enrico Rava, concerts of Bartók, Messiaen and Part, and theatre projects including Büchner's *Danton's Death*, Guy Cassier's staging of Lowry's *Under the Volcano*, and Heiner Müller's *The Mission*. This striking nine-storey, transparent building, dominating an entire block of Syngrou and mixing classical Greek architectural forms with austere minimalism, has a 900-seat auditorium large enough for a symphony orchestra or a full-blown war epic from Euripides or Aeschylus, a smaller 200-seater auditorium, an open air theatre, library, sound studio and restaurant.

Bios and the Cacoyannis Foundation sit in the Gazi/Kerameikos area, half a mile west of Omonia, and the site of a recent explosion in restaurants, bars, clubs and still more arts venues. These include The Hub, an independent contemporary art centre opened in late 2010, and, central to them all, the Technopolis arts complex, the former city gasworks that gave the area, Gazi, its nickname. In 1999 its gasometers and surrounding structures were transformed into the city's biggest arts centre, dedicated to the memory of Manos Hadjidakis and with eight of its renovated industrial spaces named after poets such as Cavafy, Palamas, Ritsos and Sikelianos. Its various venues host music and arts events through the year, and each June it is the site of Athens' most adventurous contemporary music and arts weekender, Synch, the city's very own, if smaller, version of Barcelona's Sonar. Along with local talent such as the aforementioned Biomass and Tasman, Synch has showcased international acts including Florence & The Machine, Happy Mondays, Stereolab and Tortoise.

In the past four years, this already crowded district has acquired another venue, the former Tsaousoglou furniture factory at 260 Pireos Street, now known to thousands of concert- and theatre-goers simply as Pireos 260. This huge renovated warehouse complex is the unlikely star of another unlikely renovation, the annual Hellenic Festival, or to give it its preferred title, the Athens and Epidaurus Festival. Originally a five-month programme of polite and conservative theatre and music events distributed among three main venues, the theatre at Epidaurus, the Odeon of Herodes Atticus and the relatively new (1960s) Lycabettus amphitheatre, in 2006 the festival was "dragged kicking and screaming", according to one press report, into the modern world by a radical new festival director, Yorgos Loukos. A former dancer, choreographer and director of the Marseille and Lyon Opera Ballet companies, Loukos transformed a rather staid and parochial festival into a short (two months) and very noisy international festival (it was probably Loukos who lured the likes of Pina Bausch and Robert Wilson to Athens) which can now probably outmatch any comparable festival around the world, even if its amusingly complex system of funding appears to depend in part on little old ladies playing bingo on Corfu...

Loukos has said in interviews that he was initially daunted by the prospect of grappling with Greek bureaucracy, but he managed to turn the festival on its head, corralling the likes of Dimitris Papaioannou into policy positions and expanding the event to encompass new venues and local artists as well as international names for a June and July festival that would make most arts lovers dream of having the money and time to spend two months in Athens. The 2010 programme alone had two visits by the late Bausch's Tanztheater Wuppertal and two by Wilson's second home, the Schaubühne Berlin theatre company, as well as Amsterdam's Concertgebouw orchestra, a revival of Tony Kushner's epic drama *Angels in America*, Maria Farantouri singing with saxophonist Charles Lloyd's Quartet, pianist Dora Bakopoulou playing Chopin, *tropicalismo* legend Caetano Veloso, and new stagings of Aristophanes, Euripides and Sophocles at Epidaurus.

Loukos seems to have found the secret formula for organizing a festival that is popular with both audiences and press and is using this as a means to drive through drastic changes in the event's philosophy. In 2010 he unceremoniously dumped much of its classical music content with the brusque rationale that "classical music has no appeal. Nobody goes to major names. Last year's Ravel tribute sold just 525 tickets." (Although that year still featured Chopin, Haydn, Mahler, Prokofiev, Schumann, Stravinsky, Wagner and... Ravel.)

At the same press conference where he disappointed Athens' five-hundred and twenty-five Ravel enthusiasts, Loukos also revealed some interesting statistics about the revamped festival. In the three years since he took over, an estimated three-quarters of a million people had attended festival events, and fifty per cent of that audience was in the 20-30 age bracket, twenty per cent of whom Loukos said were probably unaware of the festival's existence until a few years earlier. Most interestingly, however, he revealed some of the accounting behind the event. In 2009 it had a budget of eight million euros to spend on artists and running costs. It had funding from the government of five million, plus an intriguing tithe of nine million from the hugely popular gambling casinos on Mount Parnes, north of Athens, and the one in Corfu, where in truth little old ladies playing bingo probably only contribute a fraction of what amounts to a gambling arts tax. The festival has also secured a five year sponsorship from the country's largest bank, the National Bank of Greece. In the smoke-and-mirrors culture of arts funding, the festival is probably able to offset any losses against other accounting columns, but for Loukos to have succeeded at this point in the recent history of the Greek economy is particularly remarkable. Cities such as Berlin, London, Madrid, New York and Paris can probably claim similarly star-studded arts seasons, but it is unlikely that any has been able to marshal them under the roof of one single festival.

Nightlife

In recent years, the proliferation of restaurants, bars and clubs in the Gazi/Kerameikos area has made this the new nightlife centre of the city, with Persefonis and Voutadon Streets on either side of the small park facing Technopolis lined with outdoor terraces and busy year round. While bars and restaurants change with such frequency as to make recommendations nearly redundant, places such as The Butcher Shop (despite the English name, in fact an entirely Greek organic meat restaurant) and Mamacas on Persefonis have both taken root to the extent that they should be around for a while. It is also worthwhile mentioning another excellent restaurant, O Tzitikas kai o Mermigas—the Ant and the Cricket—on Mitropoleos Street below Syntagma, and its sister on Aeschylou Street near Monastiraki Metro (there are four spread around the city), although if you want to go broke in style, it has to be the Michelin-starred Spondi on Pyrronos Street in Pagrati. The tourist ghetto of Monastiraki and Plaka is pretty much AYOR, at your own risk, although Athenians go there too, so follow the traveller's one golden rule: eat where the Greeks eat.

The Gazi and Kerameikos area has also become the home to a newer, younger LGBT bar scene, with bars more likely to advertise themselves in the street with rainbow flags than the older, more discreet gay and lesbian bars of Kolonaki and Makrigianni. Male homosexuality was decriminalized in Greece in 1951 and lesbians have never been criminalized here. Church and state have meddled in civil rights issues over the years (the former managed to annul Greece's first gay marriage, on the island of Tilos, in 2008), but native and visiting queers have found life in Athens far more amenable than elsewhere. LGBT culture in Athens is small but visible and its endearingly modest annual Gay Pride march in June attracts less than ten thousand revellers. Lacking the gender apartheid of many northern European LGBT communities, its queer bars are often mixed sex and there is a healthy combination of lesbian nightspots as well as the inevitable boy bars. These too are known to change at whim, although Gazi is home to one of the city's oldest LGBT bars, Sodade, on Triptolemou Street (the other old timer is Lamda, on Lembesi Street near Akropoli Metro). At last fly-by, Gazi was home to at least half a dozen LGBT bars, clubs and restaurants, including Almaz, Almodobar, El Cielo, Fou, Kazarma and Mayo. Some clubs, such as Fou, retain a men-only leather/bear policy, but most are relaxed to the extent that gender and sexual orientation are not an issue on the door.

While Athenians can match Barcelona's nightclubbers in dancing until dawn and beyond, they are also ardent daytime boulevardiers or flâneurs, at least in the pre-Walter Benjamin sense of city stroller and café habitué, to the extent that the visitor might wonder if half of Athens is permanently on holiday. Most in those Gazi terraces or outside the cafés of Exarheia or Kolonaki are either on a break or off work, or on their way to or from the same. Coffee with friends, preferably outdoors, is a tradition dating back to the New Athens of its Belle Epoque era, and probably reaches its apogee in the astoundingly expensive Zonar's *zaxaroplasteio* (pastry shop), with seats and tables wrapped around Voukourestiou and Panepistimiou Streets outside the Attica department store. A quieter, and cheaper, coffee can be found at the numerous bars and cafés in and around Exarheia Square, particularly the Floral café-bookshop, where musicians, writers and wannabes dawdle. Exarheia was unofficially twinned with wartime Beirut by the international press following the 2008 riots, when in fact it is a leafy community square (although one sometimes garlanded with anarcho-syndicalist banners) more comparable to Greenwich Village, with climbing frames for kids and games tables for adults, popular with students from the nearby university buildings and a few minutes' walk from the Archaeological Museum. It is handy for Exarheia's many bookshops, music stores, clubs, galleries, boutiques, at least two of those summertime outdoor cinemas and restaurants such as the long-established Barbara's Food Company on Benaki, the excellent Spanish eaterie Salero on Valtetsiou, and across the street and next door to the Riviera cinema, the upmarket courtyard restaurant Giantes. If this writer were still a city animal, he would dream of an apartment in Exarheia.

From Astronomy to Zoology: Museums

There are still more attractions between the sidewalk cafés and extreme nightlife pursuits to be shared with the Athenians, ranging from the sublime to the ridiculous. Beyond the famous Archaeological, Benaki and Cycladic Museums, there are dozens of others, most within walking distance of the city centre. All are listed at the city's official website, Breathtaking Athens (www. breathtakingathens.com), the most reliable web source of tourism information. Depending on interest and available time (bearing in mind that some museums close one or two days a week, and others shut mid-afternoon daily) the visitor can take in specialist museums on subjects from astronomy to zoology. Athens has no city-sized zoo as such, although the Attica Zoological Park, opened as a bird sanctuary in 2000, has been slowly expanding to include scare-the-kids attractions such as large snakes and reptiles, wolves, bears and other Greek fauna, and most recently big cats and primates. The Zoological Park, near Doukissis Plakentias station on Line 3 of the Metro, is run on wildlife conservation guidelines rather than as a theme park, so visitors need not fear anthropomorphic horrors such as performing dolphins or parrots on roller skates.

Astronomy buffs visiting Athens have no fewer than three opportunities to explore *apotero diastima*, the Greek for "outer space", should the phrase ever come in need. The recently refurbished Digital Planetarium at the Eugenides Foundation on Syngrou Avenue is now one of the most advanced astronomy attractions in the world, with a 280-seater auditorium and a 72-foot domed screen also making it one of the world's largest. The National Observatory (the one built by Theophil Hansen in the nineteenth century, and perhaps comparable to Greenwich Observatory) sits atop the Nymfon Hill, beyond the Acropolis on Dionysiou Areopagitou Street, and while no longer operational it houses a beautiful collection of scientific equipment it shares with the neighbouring Museum of Geoastrophysics. The astronomers themselves decamped long ago, taking a Newall refractor, a magnificent cigar-shaped mechanical beast built in 1869, with them to the working observatory fifteen miles out of town on the slopes of Mount Penteli, where they host monthly open evenings through the year.

There are alas just two zoology collections in Athens, the largest of which is the Goulandris Natural History Museum, in a leafy back street of northernmost Kifissia, and the more academic of which is the Zoological Museum of the University of Athens, some way off the Metro system out beyond Ilision Park. Both hoard more fossils and taxidermy than anyone will remember from childhood visits to the Horniman Museum or the National History Museum on West Central Park.

Closer to the centre, the Jewish Museum on Nikis Street behind the post office in Syntagma has a poignant collection of memorabilia and religious artifacts from the city's Jewish history, up to and including events in Athens and Greece during the Nazi occupation (the Jewish Museum will re-appear in another, darker, context in a following chapter). Facets of the city's military history can be seen at the National Historical Museum on Stadiou Street, in Boulanger's original parliament building, where the parliamentary chamber is preserved intact and is surrounded by displays from the War of Independence and later, including Velestinlis' fatally ambitious map of an imagined unified Greece (hung above the very desk where Adamantios Korais imagined his own unified Greece), and also at the War Museum on Rizari Street and Vassilissis Sofias Avenue, where an outdoor display bristling with jet planes in fact conceals a sober museum tracing the history of Greek warfare back to the Byzantine era. The nation's recent naval history has been moored at a dock in Palaio Faliro, half an hour by tram from Syntagma, aboard the Battleship Averof Museum, which in its original function saw action in both Balkan Wars at the beginning of the twentieth century and in the First and Second World Wars.

Before we even begin to explore the surrounding countryside, there are still more museums of art concealed in the city. The multi-site Benaki has no fewer than four satellite museums: the Islamic collection on the corner of Asomaton and Dipilou Streets in Kerameikos; the contemporary art extension at 138 Pireos Street; the aforementioned Hadjikyriakos-Ghika Museum on Kriezotou off Panepistimiou; and two museum-homes of early twentieth-century architecture and décor, the Delta House in Kifissia and the Kouloura House in Palaio Faliro. The Folk Art Museum, on Kydathinaion Street and in four other nearby buildings, has an extensive collection of artisanal design, costume, folklore and domestic and industrial crafts. The very latest addition to the ever-lengthening line of tourist destinations on Pireos Street is the futuristic Hellenic Cosmos Centre, a block away from Moschato station on the Metro, with a virtual reality presentation on Athenian and Greek history, scientific exhibits, theatre, music and performance spaces and more.

Finally, three attractions that involve rails. Athens has two railway museums, the main one on Siokou and Liosion Streets, a hike from Aghios Nikolaos Metro, and a second attached to the railway station at Piraeus, itself a handsome example of nineteenth-century railway architecture. Both museums feature vintage and contemporary rolling stock and enough technology to send enthusiasts into transports of, well, transport. Lastly, no European city would be complete without a funfair, even though London seems to have muddled by since the death of Battersea Funfair in 1974. Allou Fun Park, off the motorway toward Piraeus and best reached by bus from Omonia or Syntagma, was opened in 2001 but features old-fashioned fairground rides as well as hi-tech white knuckle ones. It opens year round, on weekday evenings and all day at weekends. After exhaustive researches that have taken this writer from Copenhagen's Tivoli to Vienna's Prater, it seems only fair to warn you that you should also expect to get very wet.

Not the Saatchi: Billionaire Dakis Joannou's mini-Hermitage of
contemporary art, DESTE

9 | Changing Faces
Migration and Social Change

A small earthquake struck Athens on the evening of 14 November 2010, although it was not the sort of seismic activity that would be picked up on the "Real-Time Seismicity" sensors in the Department of Geophysics-Geothermics at the University of Athens geology faculty, which feed an interactive map that you can explore at the department website. This quake sent pressure waves across the surface of Athenian politics, when a modest fifty-two per cent of a controversial, abstention-heavy vote elected independent candidate Yiorgos Kaminis as the first socialist mayor of Athens in almost a quarter of a century.

Kaminis' success, matching a comparable socialist victory in the traditional centre-right Nea Demokratia stronghold of Thessaloniki, stunned even his supporters in the Ecology Party, PASOK and the new Democratic Left party (DA, Dimokratiki Aristera) formed in June 2010. While the new mayor will have to cope with the perennial complaints about rubbish collection, transport, housing and employment, his appointment has shunted immigration—currently a hot topic on the streets, newspaper front pages and television screens of Greece—to the top of the list of issues that the mayor's office will have to address. It is quite possible that many Athenians still do not know just what sort of mayor they have on their hands.

Kaminis was born in New York and moved to Athens aged five, when his parents returned there. He currently holds joint citizenship. He graduated from the law school of Athens in 1980 and pursued post-graduate law studies at the University of Paris, returning to Athens to work as a lecturer and then as an assistant professor before moving on to become a research fellow in the Directorate of Studies of the Greek Parliament. He published his first book, *La transition constitutionnelle en Grèce et en Espagne*, in France under the

Hard times: Children queue for food relief in the aftermath of the Asia Minor Disaster

name Georges Kaminis, following it in 1998 with *Illegally Obtained Evidence and Constitutional Guarantees of Human Rights: The Exclusion of Evidence in Criminal and Civil Proceedings.* He is the kind of politician, then, you would want on your side when things go wrong. The same year he became Greece's Deputy Ombudsman for Human Rights and Ombudsman in 2003, resigning in 2010 to enter the mayoral election. He fought the race on a broad ticket of promising a more "meritocratic" city for all, fighting corruption and bureaucracy (he also promised to do something about that rubbish). His record as Ombudsman, negotiating in thousands of human rights cases, many of them involving immigration issues, will make him a fascinating mayor to watch.

Kaminis' appointment could not have come at a more felicitous, nor more unfortunate, moment. His election coincided with the Muslim festival of Eid, when thousands of Athenian Muslims, in the only European capital with a sizeable Muslim community but without a single mosque, celebrated in public spaces around the city, in some parts drawing hostile reactions from non-Muslim inhabitants and in one case sparking a violent street demonstration by the neo-Nazi group Chrysi Avgi ("Golden Dawn"), which that week also won its first seat on the Athens municipal council. It also came in a year when racist attacks were reported to be on the increase in parts of the city, when tensions between different ethnic groups flared on the streets and when the Jewish Museum off Syntagma Square was daubed with red Swastikas by eight attackers who, despite the presence of CCTV cameras, have yet to be caught. (As one Jewish news blogger noted, "in previous decades we always felt perfectly safe in Greece. I wonder what has gone so badly astray...") It also came during a period when Greece was making international headlines with its lamentable treatment of refugees, and when Amnesty International lodged a complaint with Frontex, the new European border patrol authority, about its decision to deploy 175 armed guards along Greece's border with Turkey—where in July 2010 alone sixteen people drowned trying to cross the River Evros into Greece. If anyone can address these problems, Yiorgos Kaminis is the man for the job, although it is not a position to be envied.

This turn of events, in one of the otherwise most adaptable cities in Europe, is doubly shocking when you consider the history of Athens and Greece, a capital and a country founded on the ebb and flow of populations across the Balkans, the Mediterranean and beyond. In the first millennium BCE, Greeks along with Muslims and Phoenicians invented Europe, helping to found Naples, Marseille, Barcelona (established in legend by Heracles; neighbouring Girona was first settled by Greeks) and Cádiz. The jury is still out on whether the Greeks—specifically Odysseus—founded Lisbon, as the Phoenicians may have got there earlier. The intervening centuries saw our notional "Greece" mixing its gene pool with those of Italian, Spanish and northern European invaders and settlers. More recent centuries saw a mass exodus of Greek economic migrants to the US, Australia and, in recent decades, Germany.

For the better part of two centuries, Athens has been the hub through which all of these populations on the move have passed. Since foreign tourists started arriving in Greece in ever increasing numbers during the 1960s, one of the key attractions for visiting here has been the abiding culture of φιλοξενία, *filoxenia*, translated simplistically as love of strangers, but more accurately as hospitality or kindness, a philosophical gift that can surprise you in the most unlikely circumstances. We might well wonder alongside that Jewish news blogger about just what has gone so badly astray…

Athens has woken up in the twenty-first century to find that almost overnight it has been shifted to a frontier point in the new Europe. Over the past two decades or so, the porous sea border between Spain and North Africa was the key entry point for people hoping to reach Europe, but as the methods of policing Fortress Europe have changed, so the focus has shifted from Morocco and the deadly beaches of Tarifa to Greece's border with Turkey and the dozens of tantalizingly navigable Greek islands a few miles from the Turkish coast. In 2007 the Greek authorities detained 112,364 illegal immigrants, mainly in the Dodecanese islands, triple the number detained in 2004 (and around about the time that a Frontex helicopter photographed a Turkish coastguard vessel craftily shepherding a boatload of refugees into Greek waters). Of the half a million or so illegal immigrants detained across Europe in 2008, the majority were held in Greece—almost half the number again of those detained in Spain. The refugees (mainly Ethiopians, Iraqis, Pakistanis and Somalis) were either dealt with in the islands (Chios, Kos, Leros, Samos and Patmos declared a state of emergency, while the refugee holding centre on Lesbos was declared a human rights scandal) or were shipped to Athens, where the system for handling refugees, particularly children, was promptly swamped. In fact, according to the Athens-based human rights observer, Martin Baldwin-Edwards, in his book *Immigrants and the Informal Economy in Southern Europe*, the Greek immigration system in the 1990s was more or less unchanged since before the Second World War, hence its inability to cope with the influx. These were precisely the sort of issues that Yiorgos Kaminis would have been addressing in his job as Human Rights Ombudsman.

The United Nations Special Rapporteur on Torture, Manfred Nowak, spent ten days in 2010 visiting refugee and asylum centres throughout Greece and his report described conditions for the men, women and children who are sometimes held in these centres for up to eighteen months as comparable to descriptions of the Black Hole of Calcutta. One of his conclusions was this: "Greece suffers from a highly dysfunctional asylum system with protection rates at first instance of almost zero per cent." Partly as a result of his report some countries, including Britain and Norway, have stopped sending refugees back to Greece despite the controversial "Dublin Regulation II" of 2003, which requires that all refugee applications be handled in the first EU country of entry. This is not, however, callousness on the part of Greece: until the recent influx, it had little need for a structured system for dealing with large numbers of immigrants. The migrants themselves do n0t particularly want to stay in Greece, either; as Costa-Gavras observed in his film *Eden is West*, they are heading for family or a new life in France, Germany or those famously gold-paved streets of London. The Dublin Regulation effectively traps migrants in a country without a system to handle them, although there is growing evidence of systemic discrimination against migrants inside the Greek asylum system: of an estimate

9,050 asylum applications in Greece in 2005, only two were granted on the first application.

This problem has particularly manifested itself in the poorer areas of Athens, where refugees and migrants (there is a distinction, even if they often travel in the same boats or trucks) are sometimes reduced to living on the streets, alongside those transnationals in and around Omonia Square and elsewhere. Greece has done itself no favours, either internationally or internally, in its inadequate and confused response to a crisis that has been shunted on to its doorstep by a brutish clampdown on the desperate trade in people between North Africa and southern Spain. There is also photographic and testimonial evidence of abuse of refugees suggesting that Greece's policing of its own land and maritime borders is in need of prompt and drastic reappraisal.

It is important to note, of course, that not all of the people flocking into Athens and elsewhere in Greece are asylum seekers or refugees. Like Berlin, London, New York and Paris, Athens has long been a multicultural city, not least with its historic Jewish community, even if ninety-seven per cent of it was eliminated during the Holocaust. Its ethnic areas are almost as famous as those of London or Manhattan. The Athenian answer to Chinatown, around Koumoundourou Square near Omonia, has grown to an estimated twenty thousand inhabitants in the past decade, although in the economic downturn this number is reported to be dwindling. Between here and Karaiskaki Square, around Metaxourghio Metro, are street after street of Bangladeshi, Indian and Pakistani businesses serving a community comparable in size to the Athenian-Chinese population. This overlaps with the sizeable Albanian community (fifty-one per cent of all immigrants) around Metaxourghio, in addition to settlements in Ano Kypseli, Ano Patissia and elsewhere. The lower reaches of Patission Street pass through various African communities, and at the top it runs parallel with the Romanian and Eastern Europe enclaves along Acharnon Street. There are also small, sometimes tiny, enclaves of Athenians born in the Congo, Cuba, Ethiopia, Gambia, Ghana, Guinea, Kenya, Libya, Madagascar, Nigeria, the Philippines, Poland, Senegal, Sierra Leone, South Africa, Tanzania and elsewhere, each with their own community organizations, cultural centres, restaurants and bars, even a few with their own print and electronic media. Periclean Athens would have presented a similar multicultural mix of people who had chosen to move their life or trade somewhere else, only smaller.

Muslim and Jewish Athens

By far the largest ethnic grouping is the city's Muslim community, at some estimates numbering over 100,000, of an estimated 500,000 Muslims living in Greece—and this in a country, like its capital, without a single functioning mosque (if you do see a minaret, such as in Ioannina, it is more likely to be attached to a tourist attraction rather than a place of worship). Actual figures for the Muslim population are hard to ascertain, as not all are represented in census figures, although there is a statistical consensus that they represent around 4.7 per cent of the national population, or less than one in twenty.

The Muslim population of Athens is complex, made up of indigenous Muslims, Albanians, Turks, East European Pomaks and Roma, as well as people from the near and Far East. In 2007 this population acquired its first (minaret-less) place of worship, the two-thousand-capacity Arab Hellenic Centre for Culture and Civilization in the southern suburb of Moschato, but that falls some way short of the requirements of the entire Muslim community, who have to worship in cafés, community centres, homes and even cellars. There have been various attempts to build mosques elsewhere in the city, supported by governments of both Left and Right, but these were often blocked by the Orthodox Church and pressure groups with perhaps overly-long memories of Greco-Turkish tensions.

Along with the other ethnic groupings, Athenian Muslims amount to less than four per cent of the overall city population, and are disproportionately disadvantaged in terms of employment, health provision, housing and welfare. Individuals such as the new mayor have been working to establish a more equitable design for living for Greek Muslims and so have ordinary Athenians and Greeks in general: in the islands, where the pressures on small local populations have become acute, there are innumerable accounts of admirable individual and organized humanitarian efforts on behalf of both the displaced and the settled.

Anyone who has lived in a large multiracial city will have found themselves, happily or otherwise, coming to an accommodation with the social contract that requires us to co-exist with our neighbours regardless of their colour, religion, politics, cuisine or musical tastes. Some even find it an enriching experience worthy of celebration, or at the very least they will discover that such differences are not fundamental barriers to co-existence. Like Amsterdammers and Manhattanites, the vast majority of Athenians are unconcernedly cosmopolitan (a word, as the paterfamilias of *My Big Fat Greek Wedding* would remind us, of Greek origin, meaning worldly or sophisticated, from the Greek *cosmos*, world, and *politis*, citizen), although there is a disturbing undercurrent of xenophobia in some quarters. The daubing of Swastikas on the walls of the Jewish Museum was merely the latest in a number of anti-Semitic attacks across Greece in recent years, following similar acts in Ioannina, Thessaloniki and elsewhere, the desecration of a holocaust memorial on Rhodes and the repeated arson attacks on a historic medieval synagogue (ironically operating as a multi-faith centre at the time) on Crete.

In 2004 the Simon Wiesenthal Center in Paris published the results of a two-year survey of anti-Semitism in Greece, although most of the examples it listed were in fact pro-Palestinian statements made by newspaper columnists and cartoonists. It did, however, highlight disquieting tendencies such as the promotion of the notorious *Protocols of the Elders of Zion* in certain Athens bookshops and the habit of some politicians and media commentators to slip into bluntly anti-Semitic language. The attacks on Jewish establishments are very probably the work of associates of far-right groups such as Chrysi Avgi, whose crude xenophobia matches that of its cohorts in Britain and Germany, to the extent that they share the same graffiti phraseology, helpfully sprayed in English. Right-wing extremists were also no doubt behind the firebombing of a Muslim café in Athens in 2009, a year in which Athens also saw a gas attack on a

Muslim centre and an attempt by a racist mob to lock a group of Muslims inside a makeshift basement mosque and set fire to it. More worryingly, Chrysi Avgi has close links to the newly-formed far-right party LAOS, lending it a thin veneer of parliamentary respectability, and while Athens may have voted for a socialist mayor, it now also has a neo-Nazi sitting on its city council. This should, however, be put in context: Britain, the Netherlands and Sweden have also seen similar far-right gains in recent local elections, as well as similar outrages on their streets.

Multiculturalism

Most Athenians and migrants live largely unperturbed by the behaviour of a small crackpot minority. The "no-mosques" street brawlers are clearly outriders for a wider, pan-European fascist movement; if the motorcycle-helmeted thugs who recently disrupted the launch of a Macedonian-Greek dictionary in Athens are anything to go by, these are religious zealots who do not see the inside of a church between one family funeral and the next. Many Athenians are actively involved in countering their behaviour and defending the city's heritage as a melting pot for cultures. Like Spain in the early decades of the Franco era, Greece may have seemed cut off from modern Europe for parts of the twentieth century, particularly during the time of the Colonels, but that did not stop the more persistent border-hoppers, from the writers and artists who beat a path for the millions of tourists who followed them in the midst of the Colonels' rule, to the half a million refugees who poured across the border to escape the chaos after the collapse of communism in Albania.

We might take a measure of the city's multiculturalism from two very simple gauges: the football teams Athenians support (football was probably invented here, in the ancient Greek ball game of *episkuros*) and the music Athenians dance to when they go out clubbing. The number one Greek football team, Athens' very own Panathinaikos, follows the recent trend of recruiting talent from wherever in the world it finds it. The club's current first squad of twenty-six players features eleven non-Greeks (including three from Spain, two from Germany and one from France) and its coach is

Portuguese. Former star players have passports issued in Austria, Brazil, Cameroon, Croatia, Denmark, Finland, Germany, the Netherlands, Norway, Peru, Poland, Portugal, Senegal, South Africa, Spain and Sweden. Panathinaikos' chief rival, the fellow Athenian team AEK, does not keep such detailed figures of players' passport details, but twelve members of its current first squad are non-Greeks and its coach is Spanish. Of its 214 or so former star players, almost half were non-Greek. You would not want to be a Chrysi Avgi football hooligan trying to explain that on the terraces of the OAKA stadium.

Athenians are even more culturally open-minded when they go out dancing. While *rebetiko* (which we will return to) dominates Greek musical culture in a way that even outstrips the influence of flamenco in Spain, young Athenians long ago adopted reggae as something they could both dance to and alarm the adults with at the same time. They have not embraced African music or jazz as much as Parisians did and still do, although these genres are still there in the clubs, alongside salsa and other Latin American forms. In the preponderance of homegrown electronica acts in the city, seen at festivals such as Synch and the new Plissken Festival at the Hellenic Cosmos centre (a festival named, it would seem, after Kurt Russell's one-eyed hero in *Escape from New York*), we would be able to trace their influences as far afield as Detroit and Düsseldorf. If we threw Xenakis into the mix, we would have to detour via the Darmstadt School as well. Go shopping in any of the five Athens branches of Public, or any of the university towns around Greece that also have Public stores, and you will find disturbingly extensive displays of Greek-language hip-hop recordings, effectively twinning neighbourhoods such as Exarheia and Psirri with their cousins in Compton and the Bronx, however much we might still puzzle over the concept of Greek-language hip-hop itself.

Rebetiko, considered by many to be the true voice of traditional Greek music, has beginnings beyond the shores of Anatolia, as the music itself attests and as bands such as Biomass, Stereo Nova and Tasman have shown in their borrowings from its instrumentation and styles. If you were to trace the origin of instruments such as the

bouzouki, the baglama and the lyra, you would find yourself standing in front of a museum vitrine containing a small single-stringed
instrument invented in Mesopotamia thousands of years ago.

We could similarly pursue Athenian multiculturalism into the
more rarefied halls of the Academy, the gallery and the library—even
into the cinema and restaurant kitchen. The buildings that house
them, not to mention those Doric columns on the Acropolis, took an
idea or two from ancient Egypt and elsewhere. Greek literature may
have given the world Homer, but later it had to say thank you (and
did) for Dostoyevsky, Dickens, Orwell, Burroughs and Pynchon. It
was happy to loan Domenico Theotocopoulos, El Greco, to Toledo,
but you will also find a debt fulsomely repaid in the city's art galleries and museums to Velázquez's Spain and Caravaggio's Italy,
Monet's Giverny and Cézanne's Provence. Athenian filmmakers
would be nowhere without Los Angeleno film noir, the French new
wave, Ingmar Bergman and Andrei Tarkovsky, Pedro Almodóvar and
Lars von Trier.

We could even, if it is not labouring a point, consider the curious
route taken by some of the great Athenian philosophers—not least
Plato, but also Socrates and Aristotle—towards the desks of Hegel,
Heidegger and Nietzsche, whose ideas were imaginatively reworked
to justify the German brand of National Socialism so admired by the
likes of Chrysi Avgi today. However badly the original ideas of Plato
and others may have been mangled on their way down the centuries,
history does record exactly how they arrived on those desks in
Germany. While the Christian churches of northern Europe were
enthusiastically building bonfires out of these heretical tracts from
the Greek past, librarians in Muslim universities and collections such
as the great Library of Córdoba were carefully preserving such works
for study and safekeeping—handy, as the Woody Allen joke goes, for
when they decided to hold the Renaissance in Italy. It was to these
texts that Athenians looked when writing a new democracy to fit
inside François Boulanger's new Parliament building on Stadiou
Street in the nineteenth century. The new neo-Nazi member of the
Athens municipal council may not like to hear this, but it was Muslim
intellectuals, and at least one homosexual, who put him there.

Recent events in Athens, such as the attempted killing of Muslims worshipping inside an improvised mosque (comparable to, and probably borrowed from, the torching of churches and congregations by the Nazis and, more recently, the US far right), may well prove to be a short-term aberration in a city otherwise noted for the ease with which it can assimilate outsiders. Certainly, the visitor will have to look hard to find evidence of this discord (even the Swastikas were scrubbed off the Jewish Museum in a matter of days). Athens is probably too large, too disorganized and too stubbornly independent to knuckle under to any regime, as the Colonels, not to mention the authors of the recent third attempt to ban smoking in public spaces, found to their cost.

10 | Spending Power
Consumerism and Consumption

I f intergalactic archaeologists ever reach Earth far into the future, they will probably excavate our shopping malls looking for information about how we lived. Shopping malls, Joan Didion's "pyramids to the boom time", offer the busy anthropologist and the lazy journalist an instant snapshot of a culture, not least the way more and more of us spend our leisure time.

Greece has come late to the malling craze, or perhaps vice versa. The mall is decline in its birthplace, the USA, where in 2010 almost half of the malls in a chain of sixty-eight owned by one company alone, First Allied, were in dire financial straits. Among Mediterranean economies, both Italy and Spain have long had a developed mall culture, the three largest being the new mega-malls at Bergamo's Orio Center, Madrid's Xanadu, which boasts an indoor ski resort and golf course, and Barcelona's La Maquinista. Italian travel agents even organize dedicated shopping tours of the country's biggest malls.

Yet Greece's dalliance with the mall is barely a decade old. Developers hail the enclosed shopping centre as a logical, organic step on from the high street, while others see more cynical forces at work. In Greece, indeed as elsewhere, the mall is more likely to be the result of creative interpretations of planning laws by clever property speculators, while the evidence so far suggests that Greece's malls may already be encountering unexpected problems.

It is both a relief and a disappointment to report that Greece's two largest malls, The Mall Athens, in the northern suburb of Maroussi, and Thessaloniki's grandly titled Mediterranean Cosmos, will offer slim pickings to those future archaeologists, although this may change with the mega-mall included in the plans for the €3.4 billion development the Chinese state-owned COSCO corporation is proposing in Piraeus. A relief because these two malls suggest that Greece has so far resisted being sucked under by the malling of Europe; a disappointment because anyone perverse enough to have become a connoisseur of malls, as Joan Didion and I have, will be underwhelmed by what either mall has to offer, although the Mediterranean Cosmos does have some splendid retro-futurist architecture and a permanent funfair across the road from the entrance that might have been twinned with Coney Island.

Both malls were opened in 2005 by the Lamda Development Company, the largest retail property developer in Greece, which also built the first ever mega-yacht marina in Greece, Flisvos Marina, a leisure, shopping and *lifestyle* pleasuredrome at Palaio Faliro outside Athens that would have had J. G. Ballard itching to set one of his novels there. Lamda is owned by "the richest man in Greece", Spiro Latsis, with a personal fortune valued at $9.1 billion when *Forbes* magazine first listed him, at 51st position, in its billionaires list in 2004; relegated to 149th in 2009 when *Forbes* rated his fortune at a paltry $3.8 billion after he redistributed parts of his wealth among his family. The Mall Athens is reached by mere pedestrians at the newly-built Neratziotissa Metro station straddling the noisy Athens-Corinth E94 motorway at Maroussi, one Metro stop up from the Calatrava arches of the Olympic stadiums at Irini.

It is a compelling place for any mall connoisseur to visit at this particular juncture in Greece's economic history, when the average Greek household has had an estimated one-third wiped off its spending power by mischief (or "fun", as one City of London trader described it) in the international money markets. This half-billion euro (current market worth) development represents the vanguard of Greece's off-high-street retail economy. Some 12.7 million people visited The Mall Athens in 2009, compared to just 8.4 million who headed for the Mediterranean Cosmos, despite the presence of that funfair, not to mention a free-standing Greek Orthodox church and a "Greek Village" inside the grounds of the development. It is interesting, if statistically meaningless, to compare The Mall Athens' visitor numbers to the three million people who are estimated to visit the Acropolis every year.

Neither The Mall Athens nor the Mediterranean Cosmos sells anything you could not find in the centre of Athens, really, although that is not the point of a mall (in fact, quite the reverse; you go to The Mall Athens to avoid the congestion and crowds of the actual Athens), but again Neratziotissa seems to be a long way to go in the hope of experiencing the "aqueous suspension of 'personality'" that Didion described in her famous essay in *The White Album*.

The Mall Athens is still too young to have travelled very far in the lifecycle of the average mall. It is estimated (by the respected daily, *Kathimerini*) to have cost €200 million to build, and is still in a particularly amorous honeymoon period with its tenants: according to a 2007 *New York Times* report, retail rentals in downtown Athens (specifically, Ermou Street) stood at around €300 per square metre, whereas mall tenants were paying on average €30 per square metre. With two hundred million euro sunk into its construction, and early tenants on sweetheart rental deals, The Mall Athens is still some way off the make-or-break stage.

The same article reported that ten other mall projects were in the pipeline for Athens, and some (such as the swank Golden Hall boutique mall, also in Maroussi and also owned by Lamda Developments) have already opened, although it is quite likely that others, such as the mall attached to the long-promised new stadium for Panathinaikos FC near Kerameikos, may have caught a cold in the current economic crisis.

This will be music to the ears of The Mall Athens' many opponents, particularly when we consider this mall's secret history, but the underlying theme here seems to be that, half a century after Joan Didion fell in love with these "toy garden cities in which no one lives but everyone consumes", the shopping mall may be proving an alien graft too far for Greece.

The secret history of The Mall Athens, still mysteriously undocumented despite strenuous efforts to air the details, is comic and disturbing in equal parts. It was originally proposed as a "Media Village" for the 2004 Olympics, but somewhere along the way the "Media Village" shrank and a proposed shopping precinct within its confines blossomed into the largest ever retail development in southern Europe. The then mayor of Maroussi, who formed a company to build the project prior to a buy-out by Lamda Developments, was later found guilty of constructing the mall without permission and sentenced to a year in prison (he paid a fine instead), but by that time the mall was already open. The mall-qua-media-hub actually opened a year after the Olympics ended and the battle over its illegal construction continues on its largely unreported way through the Greek legal system.

Local Tastes

You do not have to be a mall *flâneur* to notice one very big difference about going shopping in Athens: while its chic shopping zones are comparable to anything found in London, Manhattan or Paris, the city is dominated by local, independent retail concerns. The traditional leisure and luxury retail thoroughfares are famous and well marked, with streets such as Ermou, Stadiou and Panepistimiou running between Syntagma and Omonia Squares. Yet even here the inevitable stateless international chain stores are competing for space and customers among a far bigger cohort of native businesses, both large and small. Independent clothing stores and shoe shops still thrive in Athens, as do local, family-run supermarkets and neighbourhood bakeries and butcher shops.

This prevalence of native business extends into apparel (the countrywide Glou and Sprider mid-range clothing chains both began in Athens), domestic appliances (the Cook-Shop chain has 65 stores across Greece) and the media/entertainment chains such as Public and Metropolis. With Kotsovolos dominating electricals sales, it is only in furniture, with the Swedish-owned Ikea and the German-owned Praktiker both expanding their spread of outlets and beating off local competition, where Greek business does not dominate the market.

Which may be telling the disinterested reader more than he or she really needs or wants to know about how Athenians shop for soup, stockings or CDs. It might, however, give a measure of Greece's resistance to—or perhaps sheer impenetrability by—that peculiar form of retail cloning which has swept the high streets of Europe,

•

from Málaga to Malmö. It might also speak to the inscrutability of much Greek business practice, compounded by linguistic differences and perhaps by arcane business folkways that have yet to succumb to the rigours of EU standardization. One such Greek eccentricity is the system under which every *farmakeio*, pharmacy, operates an almost Masonic control of its market. Along with civil engineers and lawyers, pharmacists were among the closed-shop professions recently targeted by the Greek government. Greek pharmacists are licensed to sell far more medications than even their Spanish counterparts are, including medications that might normally be prescription-only in other parts of Europe. Pharmacists, like their colleagues in other closed-shop professions, guard their privileges carefully, but, perhaps with the IMF whispering in its ear, the Greek government wants to break that closed shop in the name of market "liberalization".

City of Shopping

Where Athens really impresses is in its specializations: to pluck a few from the air, shops dedicated to selling barometers, a street off Syntagma that turns itself over to the sale of Christmas lights each year, the luxury chocolatiers of Stadiou Street with prices that might elsewhere be attached to gold by the ounce, a shop on Solonos that sells nothing but books about the island of Tinos, the hole-in-the-wall heavy metal record stores that appear and disappear around Exarheia, the southern end of Servias Karagiorgi off Syntagma bafflingly dominated by shops selling beads and semi-precious stones and the mystery that makes the lower end of Athinas the place to head if you find yourself in need of an earth rotovator or an alembic still for homemade hooch. A similar mystery identifies lower Stournari Street behind the Archaeological Museum as the place to buy PC software, the middle the place to get anything photocopied and the top one of the best places to buy a synthesizer in Athens, should you feel the need. That these and other eccentric enterprises flourish in a twenty-first century megalopolis (as Attica technically is) is something to be celebrated. This shopper's Athens harks back to an era now long lost in Britain and elsewhere in Europe, a time when town centres and shopping districts were sufficiently different from each other to the extent that people travelled considerable distances for the novelty of shopping somewhere that did not resemble their own high street or shopping district.

Serious shopping, which we might define as the exchange of large amounts of personal wealth for items no reasonable person would ever really need, first arrived in Athens in the early 1950s, when international design houses such as Dior and jewellers such as Cartier began to congregate on Voukourestiou Street, a narrow street running from Stadiou near the Historical Museum up towards Lycabettus Hill. The political tenor of the era is key: the decade was dominated by parliaments of the right, led by figures such as Papagos and Karamanlis, which saw an influx of financial support, chiefly from the USA, from both the Marshall Plan for Europe and also from US companies investing in the new, trade-friendlier post-war Greece. Named after Bucharest and the Bucharest Treaty of 1913, which ended the Second Balkan War, Voukourestiou soon became home to other emporia of high-end knick-knackery, including jewellers Baccarat, Bulgari, Chopard and Van Cleef and Arpels. Bulgari was actually founded by a Greek, the Epirus-born Sotirio Bulgari, who launched his small, sparkly empire in Italy in the late nineteenth century, although the present Bulgari store on Voukourestiou only opened in 1993.

Dior, too, attracted other fashion houses such as Ferragamo, Hermès, Ralph Lauren, Luis Vuitton and more recently Dolce and Gabbana and Prada. Ladies who lunched could totter down to Zonar's, on the corner of Voukourestiou and Panepistimiou, where myth had them rubbing bias-cut shoulders with fellow members of the fabled Jet Set, and there were two theatres, the Pallas and the Odeon, at the bottom of the street. Alas, Voukourestiou went into decline in the dress-down 1970s, although some shops remained, while others relocated to Stadiou Street.

Prior to the current economic crisis, an apartment on Voukourestiou could sell for a cool €1.5 million, or thirty thousand a month in rental. Property and rental prices recently plunged by a third. Newcomers have joined the old guard in what *Kathimerini* claims is a renaissance on Voukourestiou and most still operate with the philosophy that if you need to know the price then the guard probably should not have let you in here in the first place.

A right turn on Voukourestiou and Solonos points you at the also anarchist-prone boutiques of Kolonaki, while a left heads down Solonos towards Exarheia, which is the heart of the book lover's Athens. The excellent seven-storey Eleftheroudakis book-shop on nearby Panepistimiou recently down-sized to a more modest three-storey premises a few doors along, as the economic turmoil hit what was once one of the largest bookstores in Europe, but Solonos and the streets of neighbouring Exarheia are stuffed with smaller, specialist bookstores and publishing houses. Solonos recently lost its branch of Best Book Hunters, probably the only place in downtown Athens where, should the urge prove irresistible, you could find Jacques Derrida in English (although there is another store on Lefkados Street, north-east of the Archaeological Museum). Solonos is also home to the antiquarian Stratis Fillipotis bookstore, with all those titles on Tinos alone, and a few doors down is the newer travel bookshop and café, Road. Also along the street is Le Livre Ouvert, a French bookshop that has lured the likes of Michel Houllebecq to give readings. Around the corner in Ippokratous Street both Kristaki and Tsigarida have large interna-tional sections, although Compendium, on the corners of Nikis and Nikodimou Streets off Syntagma Square, remains the oldest and best-loved English bookshop in the city. As well as a plethora of what were once called "head shops", Exarheia also bucks the trend in disappearing record shops, with a perhaps literal embarrassment of tiny heavy metal stores, as well as the long-established Microstore on Didotou Street, the most likely place to find con-temporary Greek music by the aforementioned Biomass, Coti K, Sigmatropic and others.

The retail economy of Voukourestiou and nearby shopping zones such as Kolonaki, Akadimias, Panepistimiou and Ermou was the first visible sign of conspicuous consumption in a city whose history is largely one of underdevelopment. There are numerous reasons for this, ranging from the long centuries of abandonment under Ottoman rule, to the debts incurred during the construction of the New Athens, numerous forays into expensive military campaigns in the late nineteenth and early twentieth centuries, and the ruinous drain on agriculture and industry during the Nazi occupation. To this can be added mis-management by the dictatorships of the twentieth century and by governments on both sides of the parliament.

Twenty-first-century Athens may be a city of post-modern architecture, hi-tech start-ups and avant-garde bars and restaurants, but it is also a city where a sizeable proportion of the population still remember the shopping lists they gave to friends travelling abroad to bring back things unavailable in Greece, and in a country where until recent decades some remote communities, such as small islands like Folégandros, still relied on a simple but effective barter system. In the continuing financial crisis, nearly a quarter of 15-to-29-year-olds were unemployed in 2010, a third up on 2009, and almost twelve per cent of 30-44-year-olds, half as many as the previous year. Unemployment topped sixteen per cent in 2011, with the traditional earners—males in the 30-44 bracket—the hardest hit. As the financial crisis continued through 2011, those statistics started to click upwards like the meter in a cab.

The one place unlikely ever to vanish from the Athens retail economy is the vast Varvakeios Market, also known as the Dimotiki Agora or General Market, straddling Athinas Street at Armodiou south of Omonia. Although smaller than the Modiano Market in Thessaloniki, this huge vaulted nineteenth-century fruit, vegetables, meat and fish market has become a photo attraction for visitors and also a culinary adventure with its various market trader tavernas, including, if you can find it, one concealed beneath the market and accessed through a discreet doorway near the olives section. The market is surrounded by exotic pet stores and bric-a-brac shops (it is barely a minute or two on foot from the Flea Market in Monastiraki), but also conceals another hive of contemporary art, the nine-storey Artower Agora gallery, at 10 Armodiou Street, with eight floors (one is a café) of independent galleries topped by a rooftop terrace with outdoor sculpture and views across the city.

There is one last aspect of shopping in Athens that is rarely mentioned, beyond travellers' warnings posted on travel websites, and that is the growing number of unlicensed street vendors hawking their wares on the pavements of the city. Shop owners complain that in their sheer numbers alone these peddlers of fake Rolexes, bootlegged DVDs and low-quality copies of Dolce and Gabbana handbags are in effect stealing vast amounts of potential income from bona fide traders. It is true that their pavement pitches, sometimes as large as a bedspread (handy for rolling up and sprinting when the police hove into view), are a menace to pedestrians, although the economics are complex. Both the vendors and the purchasers of these fakes exist in a parallel universe to the market for the *echt* object, which remains elusively and exclusively expensive to all but the tiny elite who can afford it. Mayor Yiorgos Kaminis has proposed an investigation of ways in which the street vendors might be licensed in controlled indoor market spaces. Quite how you license someone selling twenty-euro Rolex watches or copies of *Mamma Mia!* that only last twenty minutes is a conundrum that a legal genius like Yiorgos Kaminis may well resolve.

Of Diets and Dinnerology

The mythical Mediterranean Diet may be under attack by globalized fast food, but McDonald's is still outnumbered three to one in Athens and across Greece by the domestic fast food chain Goody's. Goody's is also matched by the number of while-you-wait sandwich and snack outlets franchised by the other major Greek takeaway chain Everest, which outnumbers Starbucks two to one in Greece.

Nor can fast food sate a country that probably eats more than it healthily should; Greeks love their *zakaroplasteia*, pastry shops, more than the Spanish do their *pastelerias*, which is why you can barely walk a block in Athens without passing one, virtually all of them family concerns with an expertise in deleteriously enticing confectionery that no chain operation could match. While supermarkets provide both a one-stop and a wider range than that indefatigable neighbourhood staple, the corner shop, many Athenians prefer to shop at their local *laiki*, street market.

The history of the Greek diet itself has almost as many variations as there are authors on Greece. The academic and historian H. D. F. Kitto, in his 1951 book *The Greeks* (a book still set on some degree courses), wrote, with a perhaps schoolmasterly humour, that the typical ancient Athenian dinner "consisted of two courses, the first a kind of porridge, and the second, a kind of porridge", adding, in similar tone, "In Homer, the heroes eat an ox every two or three hundred verses, and to eat fish is a token of extreme destitution; in classical times, fish was a luxury, and meat almost unknown." Half a century later, James N. Davidson, in his *Courtesans and Fishcakes*, disagreed: "Fish [were] treated as quite irresistible, lusted after with a desire that comes close to a sexual one." Treading a more sensible middle course, Robin Waterfield explains that "the ancient Athenian diet was austere by our standards". It consisted mainly of bread, savouries and watered wine, augmented by pulses and beans, sprats, sausages, cheese, eggs, pulses and vegetables. Meat, he writes, "would end up on your plate as the result of a sacrifice, and since sacrificial victims were almost always domesticated animals, fish rarely featured." Davidson argues that the absence of fish in records of the ancient Greek diet, particularly in Homer (an omission that perplexed even Plato), may have been a recondite joke, not least among a people who "lusted" after the choicest parts of a wide array of fish, local and exotic.

Davidson actually credits the Greeks with inventing food journalism—one of the earliest cookbooks in the Western world, *The Life of Luxury*, was written in the fourth century BCE by the poet and philosopher Archestratus, predominantly about fish. Davidson renovates one of its alternative titles, "dinnerology", to describe the philosophy of food, although like much of the history on this subject, dinnerology tended and still tends to focus on the eating habits of the privileged, literate few.

One thing seems certain about dinnerology then as now: as James Pettifer writes in his *The Greeks* (1993), "the Greek peasant's diet has changed little from antiquity." This diet consisted of perhaps 75 per cent cereals (Waterfield), which with a low protein content and the Attica Basin's history of poor harvests led to malnutrition-related illnesses, stunted growth and shortened life expectancy.

Byzantine and, later, Ottoman influence introduced Eastern ingredients, from spices to sub-tropical fruits, to the core of the Mediterranean diet of cereal, olives and vegetables.

It is only very recently that the Greek middle classes have begun to stray from classical Greek family cooking, an amalgam of indigenous regional recipes and transplants from Turkish, in particular, and Italian cuisine. Turkish and Arabic cuisines name some famous Greek staples, not least *moussaka*, *taramosalata* and *tzatziki*; Italy gifted its neighbours both pasta and pizza. In the late nineteenth century New Athens restaurateurs, like its architects, began to look to northern Europe for ideas, although the New Athens cooks had their eye on the restaurants of Paris. An eventful twentieth century sidelined Greece from most of the period's food fads, although in recent years it has caught up with fusion and nouvelle cuisine (sometimes simply phoneticized as *nea kuzina*, known in some parts as *kultúra*), at restaurants such as the aforementioned Spondi and the branches of O Tzitzigas, as well as Aneton, Apla, the Electra Hotel and others. If there is a star of the new Athenian food, it is probably Christoforos Peskias, trained by Ferran Adrià at elBulli, who won his first Michelin star at the short-lived 48 The Restaurant, and whose two new ventures, the Π-Box (as in pi) in Kifissia and its sibling at the Periscope Hotel in Kolonaki, have yet to appear on the guidebook radar.

The latest trend in Athens is the drink *tsipouro*, a relative of Cretan *raki* or *tsikoudia*, a grappa-like clear liqueur distilled from grape pomace, the residue from wine-making, drunk neat, iced or with water and usually accompanied by *mezedhes*, often simply referred to as the colloquial *mezes*, the myriad snacks and miniature meals that, in more traditional bars, *tavernas* and *ouzeris*, can, as more food arrives with new rounds of drinks, amount to a complete meal in themselves. Mezedhes (which similarly have an etymology in Turkish and Persian cuisine) actually predate the invention of tapas in Spain, credited to Alfonso the Tenth, in the thirteenth century, in possibly the first recorded social intervention against binge drinking, by a few thousand years, in the snacks eaten to pace the lengthy drinking at the classical symposia. At their best—and you are as likely to find excellent mezedhes in a small backstreet joint in Piraeus as you are in a designer bar in Kolonaki—mezedhes can actually rival the most exquisite productions of the *nea kuzina* set, and without recourse to the liquid nitrogen food processors and quantum mechanics of molecular gastronomy.

11 | The Dark Side
Slavery, Calamity and Adversity

> "It is undeniable that the Athenian economy depended crucially on the available of slave labour."
>
> Robin Waterfield, *Athens: From Ancient Ideal to Modern City*

History and the guidebooks record the monuments and lifestyles of the rich and the great, but they often overlook the engineers and workers who built the monuments and the people who made the lifestyles of the rich and the great possible. We marvel at the designs of Ictinus and Phidias as the designers and architects of the Acropolis, and possibly even the feats of engineering that lofted those huge slabs of marble from Mount Penteli into position, but little is written of the number of slaves needed to bring the marble the six miles from Penteli, or those who carried it up on to the Acropolis rock and then manoeuvred the columns and other parts into their final shape.

Slaves, who numbered perhaps a third of the Athens population of an estimated 100,000 at its Periclean peak, were essential to every aspect of Athenian life. Robin Waterfield goes on to write:

> Huge numbers of slaves were imported into Athens in the fifth century, when the empire gave both the state and individuals disposable income, until there were about 100,000 slaves throughout Attica, of whom about 15,000 worked in the mines of Laureion at times of peak demand for labour, about 50,000 in Athens and Peiraieus, in domestic employment or in factories or on various publicity duties, and about 35,000 on the scattered parcels of land owned by the rich or, again, in domestic or jack-of-all-trades employment on a farm.

Throughout the centuries of its numerous experiments with democracy, Athens relied on slave labour—the majority *barbaros*, barbarians, taken from other countries as prisoners of war, but occasionally, in times of military or financial crisis, taken from the lower ranks of Athenian society—in every aspect of its society. Slaves worked in the home, in all sectors of administration and commerce and in the military. Waterfield estimates that "probably over half the citizen population of Athens owned one or more slaves", and none of them is recorded as having any reservations about this arrangement. Slaves rowed the triremes and worked the land and dug the silver from the mines at Lavrion, the modern name for Robin Waterfield's "Laureion".

The Lavrion silver mines, in particular, were notorious as a living hell where untold numbers died while extracting the silver that paid for the Periclean project and most of the city-state's other civic and military enterprises. The silver was used to mint the *tetradrachmon*, its value, as the name suggests, equivalent to four early drachmae, which became the common coinage throughout the Greek Mediterranean. The mines were the main source of wealth through the Peloponnesian Wars, rule by Sparta and Rome, as well as successive occupations, until they were abandoned in the sixth century BCE, their remaining deposits inaccessible to the available technology. They were re-opened in 1859, when newer technologies allowed the young Greek state to resume extracting smaller amounts of silver but also larger quantities of minerals, a trade that continued until the mines were again abandoned in the 1980s.

The Lavrion mines are history's singular financial gift to the Greek economy. While Thessaloniki became the second capital of the Byzantine Empire, thriving on its trade network, and while the islands, ports and their shipbuilders dominated the maritime industry from Periclean times to the twentieth century, Athens and the mainland remained dependent largely on agriculture and trade. The shipping magnates became fantastically wealthy, as their mansions and gifts to the nation attest (although their descendents have begun to diversify into activities such as shopping malls in Maroussi) but this did not translate to the wider economy. By 1887 Greece's merchant fleet numbered over five thousand vessels, with a hundred thousand vessels a year from around the world using Greek ports. Mechanization and the Industrial Revolution did not entirely pass Greece by, but their effect was minimal. In the 1870s Piraeus and other centres of the cotton trade (Patras, Thessaloniki, Volos) employed almost fifty per cent of the industrial workforce, and the number of cotton mills increased from an initial eighteen to over a hundred by 1935, but this was largely for the domestic market in cheap clothing.

While agrarian Spain could respond to shifts in trade to make Barcelona the "Manchester of the Mediterranean", Greece remained dependent on agriculture and lesser domestic industries such as the country's gold, silver and metals mines, its sizeable lignite (brown coal) and mineral fields, armaments and the ancillary military trades, ever boosted by altercations with Turkey and unfriendly Balkan states. Greece remained poor and was about to get poorer, sparking the first waves of mass emigration, to the USA and later Australia, northern Europe and elsewhere.

Rich and Poor

In this light, the dreamed city of Kleanthes and Schaubert might begin to resemble an overly elaborate shop front for an interior that had yet to acquire either a floor or a ceiling. The lack of infrastructure in the New Athens led to a variety of crises: in housing; in public sanitation and health; in public safety and civil order. By the 1880s the lack of adequate sanitation in the poorer areas of the city produced epidemics of cholera, diphtheria and typhoid. Most of the streets away from the famous boulevards were unlit and dangerous at night. The newly formed police force was largely illiterate and untrained (and uninterested) in the law. Police torture and arbitrary arrest were common, and certain sectors of the city became known for their regular rock-throwing "stone wars" (Eleni Bastéa) between populace and police.

As in London and other booming nineteenth-century cities, Athens was often host to frank and lively dialectical exchanges between the have-nots and the haves, often conducted over the heads of the police, who were there largely to protect the latter from the former. Bandits or *klephts* thrived in the countryside, and provided many of the culprits paraded in the weekly public executions in the centre of Athens. Felons were customarily beheaded, their heads displayed on staffs in the "Mars Square", or Pedion tou Areos park, north of the Archaeological Museum.

While intellectuals such as Palamas, Roides and Papadiamantis debated the "dualism" between the forces of modernism and the desire to retain traditional identity, the Athens newspapers bemoaned the state of the streets, the lack of sanitation and hospitals, and the fact that in 1883 there were only two secondary schools for boys in a city of over eighty thousand people. Eleni Bastéa writes that "the new private mansions marked in marble the great chasm separating, still, the autochthon [native] from (some of) the heterochthon [newcomer] Greeks." It would take more than Pierre Coubertin's 1896 Olympic Games, funded by the Zappas and Averoff business clans, to paper over these cracks.

The Games happened, of course, but the cracks remained, not least after Harilaos Trikoupis made his famous declaration of bankruptcy to parliament in 1893. Greece's economy would be battered again by the Greco-Turkish War of 1897, the First and Second Balkan Wars of 1912 and 1913, its late entry (1916) into the First World War, and the three-year Greco-Turkish War of 1919-1922, which culminated in the Asia-Minor Catastrophe of September 1922 and the arrival of a million refugees in Greece, a third of those in Athens. The two Greco-Turkish wars came less than a century after the ugly and protracted end of almost 400 years of vindictive Ottoman rule in Greece, an endgame fought across Athens and the Acropolis over a period of months.

Along with the burning of Smyrna, Mustafa Kemal Atatürk's final atrocity against unarmed civilians after a series of well-documented tit-for-tat outrages committed by both sides, the wars go some way to explaining the anti-Turkish sentiments that still simmer among older Greeks today. (The two countries are friendly on paper, but Turkish airforce jets flout Greek-Turkish borders in the Aegean on an almost weekly basis, and the two countries are in delicate negotiations over the future of islands such as Kastellórizo, although the subtext here is under-sea oil reserves off Kastellórizo, rather than this beautiful if useless islet half a mile off the Turkish coast.)

The dramatic expansion of population in Athens after the Asia-Minor Catastrophe, in a city now occupied by more than ten times the numbers for which it was designed, swamped the city and also created Mark Mazower's "first genuine urban proletariat", one that, as the trespassers on Otto's front lawn had shown, was not shy about sharing its differences of opinion with authority. (In fact, we might say that its great-grandchildren can be observed out and about still disagreeing with authority today…) The living conditions that Mazower describes—families of four or five living in a single room, open sewers running through the streets and scenes of destitution that might have been copied from the pages of Dickens or Zola—produced an underclass that showed its mettle in resistance to the Nazi occupation, but proved a little more problematic when power returned to domestic tyrants.

Famine and Deprivation

Athenians might justifiably have felt abandoned by their protecting goddess when they woke up on Sunday 28 October 1941 to find themselves at war with Italy and its ally Germany. The city suffered disproportionately during the occupation, when it found itself host to another population influx, "several hundred thousand" (Mazower) in-cluding refugees, Greek ex-servicemen displaced from their posts in the wartime chaos and Axis forces who ungraciously also expected to be fed. As mentioned earlier, the Nazi presence during the years 1941 to 1944 went beyond mere "occupation" to the systematic ransacking of an entire country, from its banks, factories, mines and harvests down to shoes, clothes, heirlooms, furniture and even food looted from private homes. While Allied propaganda (from the BBC among other sources) claimed half a million died in the famine of 1941-3, a famine during which some Athenians scavenged for grass to eat while others dropped dead of hunger on the city streets, Mazower trusts in the more conservative Red Cross estimate that at least a quarter of a million died directly or indirectly as a result of the famine.

Athena similarly offered no protection when occupation evolved into civil war, when British jets started strafing parts of the city held by ELAS, and when tens of thousands ended up in concentration camps opened by post-war right-wing governments. Ironically (or perhaps not so ironically) Greece enjoyed an "economic miracle" in the post-war years, thanks largely to the support of the Marshall Plan and the devaluation of the drachma to a market-friendly level by a market-friendly government. According to the economic historian Paul Bairoch, Greece's GDP rose during 54 of the 60 years after the civil war. New technologies saw a boom in the country's sizeable bauxite (the key source of aluminium) and lignite (which now provides as much as 24 per cent of the country's electricity) industries, as well as in petroleum processing, chemicals and other forms of mining. But these non-labour-intensive industries could not halt rising unemployment figures, nor really could the economy's two biggest contributors, shipping (currently producing 4.5 per cent of GDP, and involving 4.5 per cent of the workforce) and tourism (15 per cent of GDP and 16.5 per cent of jobs). Tourism, particularly, while also bolstering construction, menial employment and local businesses, has the effect of sending most of its direct income back to the overseas companies (airlines, travel companies) that control it, leaving Greek companies a thin percentage of the price of an airline ticket or package holiday. Greece is, in effect, gripped in a stranglehold by overseas travel trade interests, who tell it how long its tourism season will be and how much it will earn, and the strangulation is getting tighter. With an estimated 75 per cent dominated by "service" industries, the Greek economy has remained in almost as parlous a state as it was in the nineteenth century, when its chief export was the humble, if tasty, currant.

These are the main factors to bear in mind when considering how history delivered Greece to its post-Colonels condition: a country under almost constant occupation for the best part of two millennia; deprived of the tools necessary to compete in both industrial and post-industrial Europe; hamstrung by extreme right-wing governments and ineffectual left-wing ones (and despite much rhetoric to the contrary, Greece has never had an extreme left government); and in recent decades beset by political and financial scandals authored by both sides of the parliamentary chamber. It might also go some way to explaining recent events in Athens and Greece, which deserve a more careful reading than the headlines that have been wielded like truncheons against the Greek body politic by the international media.

※

Something very strange happened in Greece in recent years, a series of events that resulted in what we might regard as a failing in basic humanity among observers elsewhere in Europe and beyond. Even before the financial crisis appeared on the nation's audit books in October 2009, Greece and its capital were being written out of the Europe that those nineteenth-century Athenian architects and town planners had so aspired towards. This began in December 2008 with the death, mentioned here earlier, of Alexandros Grigoropoulos, shot dead by a policeman when Grigoropoulos and a group of friends were confronted by a police patrol in a side street in Exarheia during one of Athens' not infrequent student and activist demonstrations. These demonstrations have a fairly established historical precedent, not least in the 1973 student uprising at the Athens Polytechnic, an event that is foundational to the creation myth of modern Greek democracy, but also in earlier events, such as the 1903 riots outside the National Theatre over its production of a demotic-Greek version of Aeschylus' *Oresteia*, possibly the world's first ever riot inspired by a linguistics dispute.

Demonstrations are commonplace in Athens, and anyone from elsewhere who has found themselves caught up in the banner-waving crowds that swarm along Vassilissis Sofias Avenue towards Syntagma Square will probably have found the spectacle a rather quaint reminder of how people used to voice their differences else-where, in the Paris *événements* and in Grosvenor Square, and in later demonstrations against anything worth demonstrating about. Even at their most boisterous, these normally good-natured events rarely match the ferocity of events such as Britain's Brixton and Toxteth riots, London's Poll Tax riots, the disturbances in the Paris *banlieues*, the battles in Kreuzberg and elsewhere in Berlin and Germany, or indeed the various G8 actions around the world in recent years.

When angry mobs appeared on the streets as news of the Grigoropoulos death began to spread, first beyond Exarheia, then beyond Athens to thirty other Greek cities and towns and then to other European cities, it was clear that something else was at work. In Greece it was often put down to "anarchist" ringleaders, or that small band of activists who seize every opportunity to start a fight with the police, although more sober observers suggested that something more profound was behind the actions. They pointed to soaring youth unemployment figures, widespread frustration and resentment at the lack opportunity in the job market and a crisis in graduate employment that was driving a new generation of Greece's best and brightest into a massed youth exodus abroad.

International reports of the December 2008 events suggested, however, that Greece in general, Athens in particular, and the ground zero of Exarheia especially, were teetering on the edge of the apocalypse. When the riots happened again around the first anniversary of the Grigoropoulos killing in 2009, amid breaking news of the financial crisis facing the new PASOK government, the doom-laden headlines came out again. This time, however, they were tinged with a spitefulness that veered between unseemly *schadenfreude* and unapologetic racism. Calls by right-wing German politicians for Greece to sell the Acropolis or its islands to pay off its debts were repeated with glee by newspapers such as *Bild*. The weekly German news magazine *Focus* ran its famous Venus de Milo cover, with the iconic statue Photoshopped into flipping the middle finger at the end of a newly-acquired arm alongside the headline "Betrüger in der Euro-Familie", "Betrüger" lending itself to translation as cheat, swindler or fraudster. In Angela Merkel's new conservative Germany, *Focus* not only defended its de Milo cover but repeated it a few months later, the offending digit this time Photoshopped into a beggar's open hand alongside the headline, "Griechenland und Unser Geld!"— "Greece and Our Money!"

As the scale of the Greek financial crisis became known, the international press began to conflate it with the Grigoropoulos riots, several strikes by a variety of professions targeted by the govern-ment's new austerity plans and general strikes called by trade unions and political parties, as well as unrelated events such as the annual 17 November parades, normally peaceful affairs in which even school-children are encouraged to participate in a memorial day for the his-toric 1973 student uprising in Athens. What they conflated it into was an eye-catching, if inaccurate, newsflash about the collapse of a civilization—the collapse, moreover, of the civilization where western civilization was meant to have begun.

The footage of well-prepared black-clad teens hurling Molotov cocktails at Special Guard riot police was certainly dramatic, al-though however photogenic these outrages were, they were still only a small part of a much wider, and usually well-behaved, current of popular protest against the rupture of the social contract by former government ministers in cahoots with a New York investment bank.

As the PASOK government scrambled to meet IMF demands for austerity moves to staunch the crisis, cutting pensions, welfare, public sector salaries and services, while the super-rich were clink-ing glasses on their super-yachts in Piraeus, so the demonstrations became angrier. They reached a disturbing extreme when during a general strike and demonstration against the austerity measures in Athens in May 2010 three employees at a branch of the Marfin Egnatia Bank on Stadiou Street died from asphyxiation after pro-testers (in fact believed to be one protester, young, possibly female) hurled incendiary devices into the building.

The deaths sparked an international outpouring of revulsion, particularly when one was named as pregnant thirty-two-year-old Aggeliki Papathanasopoulou. Blame was swiftly apportioned to the masked "anarchists" on the periphery of the demonstration, although members of both the KKE and the left-wing coalition SYRIZA claimed in parliament that the bombings were the action of far-right agents provocateurs, possibly with police connivance, and there were indeed reports of right-wing activists being chased off from at-tempting to join groups on the demonstration. A widely-circulated statement, allegedly from a Marfin employee, accused the bank of multiple failures in safety provisions, adding that workers were forced to work during the strike or risk losing their jobs. The bank denied any safety failures or coercion of staff, but the daily *To Vima* published a health inspection report which found, among other criticisms, that the one emergency exit at the bank was locked and that survivors only escaped through a door left open by chance.

The bank employees' union also staged a strike, blaming both the banks and police for failing to protect its members. More than a year later, the perpetrators of the Marfin Egnatia Bank bombing had yet to be identified from CCTV or news footage from the day, or from eye-witness reports from outside the bank. It remains a mystery why a bank on a main thoroughfare in a city known for its sometimes rowdy demonstrations should require staff to remain at their desks when a large and angry protest against the banking system was about to pass by its front door, when most similar organizations in Athens had rolled down their shutters and sent their staff home.

The deaths at the Marfin Egnatia Bank gave everyone, even the anarchists, pause for sober thought and the bank itself quickly became an ever-growing shrine of flowers, candles and toys left for Aggeliki Papathanasopoulou's child. They also reignited incendiary bouts of Greece-bashing in the international press, particularly as the possibility of a debt "default" became more and more likely. Some of this went beyond reasoned comment and entered the realm of unabashed racism, or what Edward Said described as "Orientalism" in his book of that name. It set the tone for much of the international media narrative on Greece, as the Indignants set up home in the newly-founded people's republic of Syntagma Square, much as the trespassers had done under King Otto's bedroom window in 1843, while intermittent strikes rolled through the spring into summer and the Papandreou government found that the space between the rock and the hard place was beginning to shrink.

The Indignants themselves, at least those camped out in Syntagma Square, rarely numbered above a few hundred, and even when tens of thousands joined them in the nightly denunciations of "IMF Employee of the Year!" Papandreou and his colleagues inside the parliament building, this wasn't much of a turnout for a city of over four million people. Nor, to date, have any of them thought to get on the Metro to take their protests to the mansions of the rich in places like Kifissia, or to the super-rich still clinking glasses aboard their super-yachts in Piraeus. The Indignants became a symbol of the nation's wider feelings of anger and despair, much as Naomi Klein observed, in her book *The Shock Doctrine*, whenever IMF representatives appear in similarly troubled economies in Eastern Europe, the Far East or South America to administer the "shock therapy" treatments of Milton Friedman's Chicago School of economics, which Klein described as "disaster capitalism". In her book, Klein outlined something akin to Elisabeth Kübler-Ross' famous five stages of trauma—denial, anger, etcetera—as experienced by people who find that the price of a loaf of bread can increase by a thousandfold after "the Chicago Boys" have been in town. On the Klein/Kübler-Ross scale, most Athenians, and Greeks, now seem to be somewhere between stages four—depression—and five—acceptance. But even when, in July 2011, a further EU agreement was reached to assist Greece, mainly as part of a much wider attempt to defend the euro and the peripheral European economies against yet more assaults by the "markets", few Athenians were cheering. The deal was described as a "new Marshall Plan" for Greece, an idea that, uncannily, had been proposed by Mark Mazower in a widely-cited *Guardian* essay a week earlier and followed similar comments by the Nobel laureate economists Paul Krugman and Joseph Stiglitz.

Most Athenians knew that even these measures were only temporary and would at best cover the exorbitant interest rates levied on the country's spiralling debts to the "markets". Some might have agreed with the low-budget documentary *Debtocracy*, a million-plus-hits internet phenomenon that was shown on an improvised screen in Syntagma earlier in the summer, which argues that Greece has been manouevred into a position of "odious debt"—and not for the first time in its history. Others might have had a presentiment of what the poet Stratis Haviaras glimpsed when he wrote his introduction to the *Eighteen Texts* in 1970, describing Seferis and his compatriots as Greeks "haunted with the same frightening vision: the extinction of the Greek people, or worse, of their humanity".

Slight of hand: The Aganaktismenoi, Indignants, send a rude message to parliament

12 | Surroundings
Suburbs and the City's Hinterland

W hile recent efforts to reduce both pollution and congestion in the city have been at least partly successful,
Athenians still expend great effort in escaping the noise
of the streets and the high summer heat: August can see Athens
almost deserted of its native population, some of them fleeing as far
as half way down the Mediterranean. Yet even in the heat of summer
the city has hidden pockets of peace and calm, as well as others
within striking distance.

Parks and Gardens
Kleanthes and Schauberts' dream of a garden-city modelled on
Versailles was compromised by financial constraints almost as soon
as it began to take shape on the ground, with building developments
consuming many of the squares and gardens that had been planned
to give the new city light, air and greenery. A small green lung
remains at the centre of the city, however, in the National Garden—
Otto's former back yard, behind the Parliament building and accessed from gates on either Vassilissis Sofias or Vassilissis Amalia
Avenues. It is also connected to the neighbouring Zappeion Hall
gardens surrounding Theophil Hansen's neoclassical Zappeion Hall,
built by the wealthy Zappas brothers for the 1896 Olympics and
used nowadays as an exhibition space and venue for public events. At
a combined size of roughly eighty acres, they are barely a fifth the
size of Hyde Park and a tenth of Central Park, although these differences level out when compared to the population they serve.

The latter garden is the more formal of the two, with manicured
vistas and statuary of poets and politicians, while the former is more
of a city centre neighbourhood space, used by families, joggers and
commuters avoiding either traffic or the Metro, with koi and terra-

pin ponds, a children's zoo, temporary sculpture exhibits and a *kafenion* under a pergola. It is also a very pleasant option for crossing between various tourist destinations in the city centre, or simply taking a break between museums, handy for the neighbouring Temple of Olympian Zeus and, a few blocks on, the entry to the Acropolis sites.

The Acropolis itself is probably the one outdoor attraction that heaves with visitors year round regardless of the weather. It is best visited early (it opens at 8am each day barring holidays) before the coach parties and guided tour groups arrive. (It has also recently become wheelchair accessible, with ramps and a lift, although users' reports suggest a wheelchair visit should be researched beforehand.) With time to spare, it is also worth approaching by the little-visited gardens on the north slope of the Acropolis, accessed by gates at Theorias and Panos Streets, offering a far more dramatic aspect of the rock than the main entrance from Dionysiou Areopagitou on the south side. The 360-degree views of city, mountains and sea from the Acropolis are bettered, if only slightly, by the higher Lycabettus Hill (at nine hundred feet, almost double the height of the Acropolis), reached by the aforementioned funicular railway on Aristippou Street—although be warned that the train travels underground so has no views. At its top sits the tiny Ayios Georgiou chapel with a restaurant and bar tucked into the rock below it.

Both the Zappeion Gardens and Temple of Zeus are a few minutes on foot from one of the least publicized public spaces, and certainly the quietest, in the city: the First Cemetery, at Anapafseos Street near Akropoli Metro. Opened for business in 1837, a few years after the new state and capital were established, it outdoes both Highgate and Père Lachaise in the grandeur and, at times, pure bombast of its neoclassical and Gothic architecture, including the spectacular mausoleum of Heinrich Schliemann, the archaeologist who discovered Troy and whose will asked that he be buried in a tomb decorated with scenes from the Trojan Wars. His neighbours include the poet George Seferis, Melina Mercouri and Jules Dassin, two generations of the Papandreou dynasty and composer Manos Hadjidakis. The most famous tomb is that of Sofia Afentaki, niece of the nineteenth-century philanthropist Georgios Afentakis, who commissioned the Tinos sculptor Giannoulis Chalepas to carve the figure of the Sleeping Maiden that adorns it.

The cemetery opens early all year round, although it also closes early in winter, and it is an almost surreally serene space in the heart of the city. It is also still an operational cemetery, but welcomes respectful interlopers. It is close to the original Panathinaiko Stadium, above which connoisseurs of inner-city suburbs will find the discreetly trendy Pagkrati district, which conceals a number of restaurants and bars (try Dompoli Street), including the Michelin-starred Spondi on Pyrronos Street. The suburbs themselves are wide open plains for the urban psychogeographer to *dérive* across, particularly the older areas such as Kifissia, Penteli and Peristeri. While the city's cultural geographers have yet to start mapping the suburbs, the Athens-based author John L. Tomkinson has produced a companion to the mythology of the Athens outlands, *Athens: The Suburbs*, which mines the secret histories of the city's periphery.

As the ride in from the airport, or the bus or train journeys in any direction away from the city, will show, you have to travel a fair way to escape the Los Angeles of the Mediterranean. The local beaches, reached by bus, tram or Metro to Glyfada, Faliro and elsewhere, are serviceable at best, although the paid-entry commercial beaches do offer facilities such as beach furniture, cafés and restaurants. The best are far away enough from the city to have earned Blue Flag awards for their beaches, such as the cliff-divers' haunt of Vouliagmeni (south of the city, and not to be confused with the same-name suburb reached by tram), Anavyssos or the sandy beaches around Kalyvia. Committed sea-bathers even head east to beaches around Marathon and Nea Makri, facing across to the island of Evvia, and even to the popular western resorts such as Loutraki, near Corinth, an hour by train from the city's "international" railway station, Larisis (Larissa), which is in fact slightly smaller than the average suburban London railway station.

At these distances, however, you might just as well aim for the quieter island beaches near Piraeus (see below). Heading away from the sea is equally time-consuming, although public transport will connect you within an hour or so to the mountain hiking regions of Parnitha, Penteli and Ymmitos, best explored off-season, away from summer heat and the risk of wild fires. Depending on weather conditions, Greece's twenty-plus skiing resorts are usually open December to April, longer in the higher and more northerly ski areas. The nearest to Athens is Parnassos, three hours by car or dedicated resort bus, which has 22 miles of ski runs along 18 different paths, 13 lifts to a variety of gradients from starter to expert, and black runs starting from as high as 7,454 feet. The next nearest is at Karpenissi, three hours in the direction of Preveza, where the smaller Velouchi ski resort has eleven runs along five miles of varying gradient, although the season here is shorter, often ending in March. There are also ski resorts in Pelion and elsewhere to the north, including a small ski centre at Vrysopoules on the slopes of Mount Olympus, accessible by train on the Athens-Thessaloniki intercity route, but complicated by connections from the nearest station to the mountain, Litochoro. These ski resorts are closer in spirit to Pradollano near Granada in Spain rather than Switzerland's Gstaad, but Greek mountain villages are renowned for their welcome—and their food.

Piraeus

Most visitors pass through Athens' largest satellite settlement, Piraeus, as fast as they can, mainly because first impressions of the four-lane highway wrapped around its vast port are usually enough to hasten the step towards where most will be headed, a ferry out to the islands. Yet Piraeus is as old as Athens itself—part of the Athens conurbation but an independent city since the middle of the nineteenth century, with its own administration and culture, even though its few historical sites such as the Long Walls were either destroyed long ago or have fallen into neglect. Given its political and economic role in the history of Athens—whenever the city's navy put to sea, it left from Piraeus, and whatever wealth accrued to the city and country, Piraeus earned it while Athens spent it—it could be said that Piraeus has a more important role in history than Athens itself, although its own siesta was even longer than Athens'. The Spartans tore down the Long Walls and many of the early developments in Piraeus at the end of the Peloponnesian War in the early years of the fourth century BCE and the Romans razed Piraeus almost completely in the first century BCE. While it roused again during the Byzantine and Ottoman periods, it only really revived in the early nineteenth century, with the birth of the new nation and its nascent maritime trade.

In its Periclean heyday, when Pericles moved the navy from Faleron to the superior moorage in the three large circular bays around Piraeus, he also commissioned the architect Hippodamus of Miletus (modern-day Milet in Turkey) to design the new city of Piraeus along what would then have been the fairly avant-garde idea of the urban grid, some 2200 years before it became a byword for modernism in northern Europe. The street plan of Piraeus today still follows Hippodamus' grid, overlaid with a partially-realized modernizing plan commissioned from Kleanthes and Schaubert around the time that they redesigned the centre of Athens itself. Two centuries of economic traffic passing through the biggest passenger port in Europe have, however, left a patina across the downtown area that renders it akin to the grimier corners of Manhattan. Some would argue, though, that you cannot have a working port without grime: just ask Aberdeen, Antwerp, Barcelona, Marseille or Rotterdam.

Piraeus was originally a small archipelago of islands, the largest of which, Munichia (today's uptown area of Kastella), became the central settlement. Silting and the growth of marshes between the islands led to the appearance of dry land bridging the new "hills" above the three harbours, around which Pericles and Hippodamus built the new Piraeus. The hills, and Hippodamus' grid, give the modern city the look of a miniature downtown Athens, not least the rollercoaster vistas of the central Vassileos Georgiou Protou ("King George I") Avenue which, like much of the grand civic and private architecture in the centre of Piraeus, dates from the Kleanthes and Schaubert era. While it followed the history of Athens (it was, as mentioned earlier, the likeliest conduit for the plague that devastated Athens at the end of the Periclean period), shifts in economic and political power saw its position of dominance across the Greek

Mediterranean overtaken early on by Rhodes and, much later, Hydra and then Syros, as these islands became larger centres of both trade and shipbuilding. At some distance from Constantinople, it was only a minor outpost of the Byzantine navy and like Athens itself it was abandoned to whatever local trade might subsist here, mainly a small fishing fleet, despite failed attempts to repopulate it with settlers from Hydra and elsewhere. It was only in the 1830s, with the dramatic expansion of Athens and the need to modernize communications and trade, that Piraeus regained its pre-eminence as a major international sea port.

Its growth during this period, in terms of both population and wealth, actually outstripped Athens' at points, as internal and external migrants flooded into the booming port. In 1835, a year after the young Otto stepped ashore here to ride to Athens and be declared king, the new "village" of Piraeus had just three hundred registered residents, but by the following year that had risen to sixteen hundred. By 1896, the year of the first new Olympics, the population had topped fifty thousand. Thousands of visitors to the games arrived by boat at Piraeus and took the train, inaugurated in 1869, to Athens for the events. Electric lighting replaced gas in Piraeus in 1902, and two years later the railway was also electrified. By 1920 the population of Piraeus was estimated at 130,000, but that rose to 250,000 in a matter of months following the Asia Minor Disaster of 1922.

New working-class suburbs, such as Kokkinia, appeared almost overnight, laying a seedbed for the city's *rebetiko* subculture, later romanticized in *Never on Sunday*, and less bucolic displays of working-class culture—as the Nazis (per Mark Mazower's researches) and more recent homegrown dictatorships would discover. Its 2010 municipal population across outlying areas, some of the Argo-Saronic islands and, by an administrative quirk, that lonely dawdler Kythera at the bottom of the Ionian Islands, is over half a million.

The advent of steam and the growth of trade at the beginning of the twentieth century saw the first major construction projects to expand the port—an expansion that continued, with the occasional interruption, until Piraeus became today's floating city-within-a-city, which is about to grow again if the Chinese state corporation

COSCO realizes its multi-billion plans to take over much of the port. Some of those interruptions may have been beyond the control of the burghers of Piraeus—several wars in the early twentieth century, for example, both increased trade but put the port at risk of attack, particularly when aeroplanes were invented that could come and drop bombs on it, which, during the Second World War, they did—but others were of its own making. While Greece and its great shipping clans, such as the Niarchos and Onassis families, were proud and keen to lend ships to the Allies in both World Wars, after 1945 the shipping magnates were disgruntled at the levels of compensation to the extent that they moved their operations out of Piraeus. Subsequent governments coaxed them back with business stimulation plans (or, in plainer English, major tax breaks) and while relations between the ship owners and governments of any political hue have remained cordial but guarded, the port-city nowadays greets nineteen million ferry passengers each year, is one of the biggest ports in the Mediterranean and one of the top ten container ports in Europe, handling over twenty million tonnes of cargo a year. Each June it hosts the Posidonia International Shipping Exhibition, and if the Piraeus Port Authority has its way it is about to acquire a large maritime theme park as well.

The modern city of Piraeus is in many ways a more authentically Greek metropolis than Athens itself, lacking—or perhaps free from—the capital's tourist infrastructure, but with its own culture and heritage, museums, galleries, nightlife and shopping districts. The downtown area around the port is given over to the needs of the travellers and trades using the port, but uphill from the port towards the heights of Kastella the city comes into its own. The shopping district between the port, Bouboulinas Street and Vassileos Georgiou Avenue is as fancy as the streets of Kolonaki, with branches of Eleftheroudakis and Public nestling among high-end fashion boutiques and designer homeware stores. The cafés and restaurants around the smaller Pasalimani and Microlimano ports, easily reached straight up and over Bouboulina from the port, overlook what has to be a good few billions' worth of ocean-going real estate bobbing, usually unoccupied, at their equally expensive moorings. Some of these floating mansions (such as the modest 204-foot runabout *The Virginian*, yours for hire at just three hundred thousand dollars a week) are so huge they cannot enter many island harbours and have to moor out at sea instead, sending guests ashore in tenders piloted by liveried flunkies.

Uphill in Kastella are the mansions built by the wealthy in the nineteenth and early twentieth centuries, nowadays forced to cohabit with nightclubs and restaurants. The Archaeological and Maritime Museums both have extensive collections from the city's history, while a hotel map will get you to the few, rather sad, vestigial remains of Piraeus from the days of Themistocles and Pericles, as well as from the Roman occupation. The city even has its own, small, rock culture, with venues such as Amerikaniko and La Rocka, while the nearby Peace and Friendship Stadium built for the 2004 Olympics sees occasional mega-events from stadium acts such as Jean-Michel Jarre, Madonna and Scorpions. In theory at least, the rock stars share dressing rooms (although U2 stayed uptown, at the OAKA stadium) with the arena's regular occupants, Piraeus' number one football team, Olimpiakos—the third in the Greek football triumvirate with AEK and Panathinaikos.

Piraeus is also home to an unusual architectural feature that, with funding, luck and planning permission, may soon transform the face of greater Athens. Built in 1972, "topped out" but never completed to operational standards, the derelict Piraeus Tower looms 275 feet and 22 storeys above the port. After the Athens Tower One block north of the city, which rises 337 feet and 28 storeys, it is the tallest building in Greece, all the more noticeable because nothing has been built of a similar size since the 1985 Building Code forbade any further skyscraper projects in this earthquake-prone region. Apart from a brief period when its lowest two floors were used for shops and offices the "sleeping giant", as it is known, has mouldered on the harbour front for nearly forty years, like a building wishing it could fall down.

Several plans to either renovate or demolish it passed through the Piraeus authorities but became entangled in either red tape or funding problems. For much of its life it has been used as a gigantic advertising billboard, hung with images ranging from a witty *trompe l'oeil* flying saucer for a German electronics corporation, complete with a shadow suggesting it was buzzing the building itself, to a mobile phone ad featuring an enormous 22-storey photograph of the footballer Cristiano Ronaldo, gazing out to sea like an improbable latter-day Colossus of Rhodes.

In early 2010, the magazine *Greek Architects* announced a competition for its readers to completely re-imagine the building, with height and ground plan limited to the form of the original structure, but space above street level to let the imagination run wild. There was no promise that the winning design would be built, only five thousand euros as first prize and a time limit of just three months for designs to be entered, but 380 proposals were submitted from 44 countries around the world. The proposals (you can see them at http://www.greekarchitects.gr/competition2010/piraeus) ranged from the whimsical—one resembled a 22-storey molten candle—to the mischievous; the "Piraeus is Dead" proposal simply sprayed that graffito across a contrived image of the building torn down to its ground floor. Some resembled the colossal glass wardrobes of Canary Wharf, others the Chippendale-topped post-modern towers of Wall Street. Many took nature as a theme; borrowing ideas from the sails of the Burj al-Arab hotel or frozen wave forms breaking over the building's core vertical rectangle. Quite a few approached it as a vast set of traffic lights, with different floors flashing ice-lolly colours day and night, while others made it disappear behind mirrored exteriors reflecting the sky. There were also a lot that borrowed from Gaudí's La Pedrera in Barcelona and covered the building with grass, plants, trees and even whole gardens cantilevered out into space. A few wanted to turn it into a bird feeder, with sloped or stepped sides planted with flora that would attract passing avian flocks.

A particular personal favourite, while eco-unfriendly in its energy demands, imagined untold quantities of water being pumped up to the 23rd floor roof to cascade back down into pools below like a four-sided Niagara Falls. That design actually won second prize, beaten to first by a "greener" conventional skyscraper sheathed in a gossamer-like lattice studded with thousands of rods (making it look like a larger version of the British pavilion at Expo 2010 in Shanghai) bristling with artificial "leaves" that will harvest wind energy from outside the building. The overall effect is like a much taller version of the transparent Onassis Cultural Centre in downtown Athens, and if the winning "Windscraper" design, by New York architects HWKN, is ever completed, it will be the most extraordinary building built in Greece for more than two thousand years.

Out to the Islands

Most visitors to Piraeus, including Athenians from up the other end of Pireos Street, have been too busy to notice Ronaldo up there (he came down in 2010) as they headed for a boat out to the islands. Few tourists realize how close Piraeus is to Athens, barely half an hour by Metro, bus or cab, and just how close some of the islands, particularly the "home group" of the Argo-Saronic islands, are to Piraeus: just thirty minutes by regular ferry to Salamis (ten if you take the commuter ferry from Perama) and around ninety minutes to tiny, blessedly car-free Hydra. Virtually all of the islands can be reached on a day or half-day round trip, although ferry schedules thin out in winter, as do the number of amenities open on the islands in the off-season. Most home group ferries leave from near Gate Nine of this huge port, where the lengthy voyage out through the various basins will give you an idea of just how large the modern Greek maritime business is.

Some, like Salamis, just one nautical mile off the coast of Piraeus, are almost suburbs of the city, although far more appealing than the traffic-harried streets of most of suburban Athens. Salamis has a history tracing back to the famous sea battle of 480 BCE and it is the birthplace of the playwright Euripides. Its more recent history, however, has been rather more prosaic. Unregulated development of both housing and industry, begun under and with the blessing of the Colonels, has left the Athens-ward side with a pollution problem, although there are continuing projects to counter this. Away from the coastal developments, however, the island rises into forest and mountain, with pristine country and coastal villages. Its population of 31,000 is estimated to increase tenfold in summertime, when Athenians flock to its main resort, Agios Nikolaos, and the beaches of Vasilika, Peristeria and Steno, where the poet Angelos Sikelianos had a summer home, converted into a museum a few years ago, and wrote much of his poetry there. The capital is modern but has some fine neoclassical architecture, and buses and sea taxis ply between here and most of the beaches.

At seventeen miles from Piraeus, but still only forty minutes by high speed ferry, Aegina is far enough from Athens to start resembling a real Greek island, but still close enough to offer the facilities of the city, even in mid-winter, when up to twenty ferries a day run between Piraeus and Aegina Town. It is larger than most Greek islands: its thirty-four square miles rise to the peak of an extinct volcano, Mount Oros, with the interior dominated by woodland or agriculture, mainly the island's main crop, pistachio nuts. Its history dates back to Mycenaean times, with many Minoan discoveries excavated as well, although its most notable antiquities, such as the Temple of Aphaia and the ruined Temples of Apollo and Zeus, date from the first century BCE. It was a major sea power in the fifth century BCE, rivalling and even skirmishing with its neighbour on the eastern horizon. Over the centuries it was overrun by the Ottomans, Franks and Venetians and played an important role on the naval front in the War of Independence.

The capital has an impressive cathedral and monastery, as well as a small archaeological museum and well-restored examples of architecture from the nineteenth century and earlier. The island's main resort, Aghia Marina, is a full-on seaside resort, with burger joints and cocktail bars to rival Corfu or Rhodes, but island buses and sea taxis also reach quieter harbours such as Portes and Perdika, which is linked by a short boat ride (perhaps out of reach on a day trip) to the beautiful, tiny deserted island of Moni.

Both Aegina and Piraeus are connected to the larger, far quieter Agistri, ten minutes from the former and forty-five from the latter, with six ferries out of Piraeus a day even in deep winter. Agistri has no notable history but is popular with Athenians and foreigners alike, as its distance from commuter connections has protected it from the development on Aegina and Salamis. Some of its larger resorts, such as Skala, have large international beach hotels, while smaller settlements above pebble beaches backed by pine forest are comparable to Ionian islands such as Ithaca and Paxos.

Some ferries out into the home group also stop at Methana, but this dramatic peninsula is in fact part of the mainland, a dormant volcano last heard from two thousand years ago. Neighbouring Poros, thirty miles and an hour out from Piraeus, could be part of the mainland as well—a channel just two hundred yards wide separates it from the mainland town of Galatas, but ferries and other craft favour this protected channel so it is unlikely to ever acquire a bridge. The island is small, just twelve square miles, but mountainous. Most of its satellite settlements are beyond the reach of a day trip, although the port and island capital is a classic and beautiful Greek island harbour town, with handsome nineteenth-century mansions stacked up hills overlooking harbour and mainland. At this distance from Piraeus, however, you might as well press on another half hour to Hydra, which is sometimes only ninety minutes from Piraeus on a direct hydrofoil.

Hydra lost its status as the ultimate bohemian Greek island hangout, where Leonard Cohen would sit writing at quayside tavernas and Sophia Loren found her sunken boy on a dolphin in the 1957 film of that name, decades ago. Nowadays it is sold as the "Aegean Hamptons" by estate agents who expect you to have a million in your pocket if you want to be taken seriously, while its habitués are more likely to be wealthy Athenian lawyers, fashion models and pop stars. Yet whoever may be snapping up its real estate, that cannot detract from the charm of its magnificent steep-sided harbour, the architecture of its massive *archontiko* mansions giving a measure of the fortunes it amassed from shipbuilding and trade over the centuries. Its importance in Greek history—not least as the childhood home of Bouboulina Laskarina, the heroine of the War of Independence (although she is nowadays more associated with her later residence on neighbouring Spetses) who names streets across Greece—is recorded in its large municipal museum on the quay.

While there are smaller settlements outside the town—including Vlichos, where a thirty minute stroll west from the port will be rewarded by a trio of excellent tavernas with stunning views of surrounding islands—Hydra harbour *is* Hydra, although its mansions long ago marched over the hill to the small neighbouring port of Kamini. (Kamini is also home to the new DESTE Foundation museum in the island's old slaughterhouse; the most recent featured artist was Maurizio Cattelan, famed for his sculpture of Pope John Paul II felled by a wayward meteorite.) Hydra has at least half a dozen boutique hotels and the bars and restaurants along its waterfront throng with visitors throughout the season. It is close enough to Athens to make it popular at weekends for a swim and a leisurely lunch on the quayside in time for the ferry back. In high season and at weekends the ferries are extremely busy, but as these are almost as regular as buses during the tourist season you are bound to get on one eventually. While you may have to queue, quite literally, to get on and get off Hydra, anyone with time and a mind for a sea journey while in Athens should consider a trip here.

By contrast, Spetses, the last island in the archipelago and at least another forty minutes on from Hydra, over two and a half hours from Piraeus, is probably just the wrong side of a day-trip's length, which would offer little more than time to explore its dull port. The pleasures of its interior and more distant beaches, which provided an ungrateful John Fowles with a backdrop when he set *The Magus* here, are beyond the reach of the day-tripper.

Casual observation would suggest, however, that Athenians also use Piraeus to strike out even further at weekends, sometimes as far afield as the fantastic beaches of Sifnos and beyond. Mykonos and Santorini, some five hours and eight to twelve hours respectively by ferry, are better reached by aeroplane, although parts of this book were written at the end of the 22-hour overnight ferry journey to far-flung Kastellórizo…

Crime watch: Detail from the British Museum's Parthenon Marbles, taken from the west frieze of the Parthenon

Further Reading

Non-fiction

Eleni Bastéa: 'The Creation of Modern Athens: Planning the Myth' (Cambridge University Press, 2000)

Thomas Cahill: 'Sailing the Wine-Dark Sea – Why the Greeks Matter' (Anchor Books, 2004)

Vangelis Calotychos: 'Greece: A Cultural Poetics' (Berg Publishers, 2004)

Jacques Derrida: 'Athens, Still Remains' (Fordham University Press, 2010)

John Freeley: 'Strolling through Athens' (Tauris Parke, 2004)

Stathis Gourgouris: 'Dream Nation: Enlightenment, Colonization and the Institution of Modern Greece' (Stanford University Press, 1996)

Edmund Keeley: 'Inventing Paradise' (Northwestern University Press, 2002)

John S. Koliopoulos & Thanos M. Veremis: 'Greece – The Modern Sequel' (Hurst & Company, 2002)

Michael Llewellyn Smith: 'Athens: A Cultural and Literary History' (Signal Books, 2004)

Mark Mazower: 'Inside Hitler's Greece' (Yale University Press, 1995)

Mark Mazower (Ed.): 'After the War Was Over' (Princeton University Press, 2000)

James Pettifer: 'The Greeks' (Penguin, 1994)

A. G. Schwarz, Tasos Sagris, Void Collective: 'We Are an Image from the Future: The Greek Revolt of 2008' (AK Press, 2010)

John L. Tomkinson: 'Athens: The Suburbs' (Anagnosis Books, 2002)

Karen Van Dyck: 'Kassandra and the Censors: Greek Poetry Since 1967' (Cornell University Press, 1997)

Robin Waterfield: 'Athens: From Ancient Ideal to Modern City' (Basic Books, 2005)

Fiction:

Apostolos Doxiadis & Christos H. Papadimitriou: 'Logicomix: An Epic Search for Truth' (Bloomsbury, 2009))

Dimitris Lyacos: 'First Death', 'Nyctivoe', 'Z213: EXIT' (Shoestring Press, 1996, 2005, 2010)

Amanda Michalopoulou: 'I'd Like' (Dalkey Archive Press, 2008)

Alexandros Papadiamantis: 'The Murderess' (New York Review of Books Classics, 2010); 'Tales from a Greek Island' (Johns Hopkins University Press, 1994)

Ersi Sotiropoulos: 'Zig-Zag Through the Bitter-Orange Trees' (Interlink Books, 2006); 'Landscape with Dog, and Other Stories' (Clockroot Books, 2009)

Vassilis Vassilikos: 'Z' (Gallimard, 1972), 'The Few Things I Know About Glafkos Thrassakis' (Seven Stories Press, 2003)

Poetry

Constantine Cavafy: 'The Collected Poems' (Oxford University Press, 2008)

Constantine Cavafy, Odysseus Elytis, Nikos Gatsos, George Seferis and Angelos Sikelianos: 'A Greek Quintet' (Denise Harvey, 2000)

Peter Constantine, Rachel Hadas, Edmund Keeley & Karen Van Dyck (Eds.): 'The Greek Poets: Homer to the Present' (W. W. Norton & Company, 2010)

Odysseus Elytis: 'The Axion Esti' (Anvil Press, 2007)

Nikos Gatsos: 'Amorgos' (Anvil Press, 1998)

George Seferis: 'Complete Poems' (Anvil Press, 1995)

Angelos Sikelianos: 'Selected Poems' (Denise Harvey, 1995)

Further Reading
Websites

About: http://aboutt.gr/
The "art/music/poetry/books" space in Miaouli Street, near Monastiraki Metro station.

Theo Angelopoulos: http://www.theoangelopoulos.gr/
One of two "official" Angelopoulos sites (the other is .com), this is the more comprehensive, in seven languages, and with excerpts from many of the films.

Athens Planetarium: http://www.eugenfound.edu.gr/
The planetarium at the Eugenides Foundation is one of the largest, and most advanced, in the world.

Antifrost Records: http://www.antifrost.gr/
Site, with sounds, for the label that is home to Coti K, Mohammad, Nikos Veliotis and others.

Athens Arts Ensemble: http://www.athensartsensemble.com/
Information, music and video of the classical group who also include The Cure, Massive Attack and Porcupine Tree among the things they love.

Athens Biennale: http://www.athensbiennial.org/AB/en/ENintro.htm
Website for the past two biennales, with news of upcoming events.

Athens tourism I: http://www.breathtakingathens.com/
The best of the official websites.

Athens tourism II: http://www.athensguide.com/
The best of the unofficial websites.

Benaki Museum: http://www.benaki.gr/
Trilingual (English, Greek, Spanish) site for the various Benaki projects across Athens.

Bios: http://www.bios.gr/
Bilingual site for the cutting-edge downtown Athens music, arts and performance space.

Michael Cacoyannis Foundation: http://www.mcf.gr/en/
Bilingual site for the performance centre founded by the veteran film director.

Debtocracy: http://www.debtocracy.gr/indexen.html
The English-language version of the independent Greek documentary on the current crisis.

DESTE 'Monument to Now': http://www.monument-to-now.gr/
An interactive archive of some of the more outlandish pieces from the gallery's 2005 show, all from the Dakis Ioannou collection.

Maria Farantouri: http://farantouri.gr/
Bilingual site with information, music and videos from the singer's archives.

Gagarin 205: http://www.gagarin205.gr/
Home of the premiere Athens rock, film and performance venue. Recent attractions included Echo & The Bunnymen, Swans, Tricky and Wire.

Greek Film Centre: http://www.gfcdigital.gr/
English, French and Greek language site with histories, stills and excerpts from hundreds of classic and contemporary Greek films.

Manos Hadjidakis: http://www.hadjidakis.gr/
Bilingual site dedicate to the life and work of the composer.

Hellenic Electroacoustic Music Composers Association:
http://www.essim.gr/
The association's members list has links to some of the *many* electronic composers in Greece.

Dimitris Lyacos: http://www.lyacos.net/
Information, excerpts of texts and also videos of performances related to the writer's work.

National Book Centre: http://www.ekebi.gr/
Celebrating Greek literature, with an online literary magazine, *Ithaca*.

Megaron Mousikis concert halls: http://www.megaron.gr/
Multi-lingual site for the city's answer to London's South Bank Centre or New York's Lincoln Center.

National Museum of Contemporary Art: http://www.emst.gr/
Greece's largest contemporary art museum, currently housed in a temporary home near the War Museum.

National Theatre of Greece: http://www.n-t.gr/
Bilingual site with information on current and previous productions, as well as NTG projects beyond its Athens base.

Onassis Cultural Centre: http://www.sgt.gr/
The startling see-through building on Syngrou has now launched a programme of art, music and theatre.

Orila music: http://www.orila.net/
An atelier music/art-object project producing limited editions of Athenian experimental music in limited editions in alarming copper sleeves, hand-painted antique Walkmen and other conceptual pranks reminiscent of early Factory Records.

Dimitris Papaioannou: http://www.dimitrispapaioannou.com/
Bilingual site with information, images and films from the dramatist's works.

Piraeus Tower: http://www.greekarchitects.gr/competition2010/piraeus
The *Greek Architects* magazine site with all the designs submitted in the competition to redesign the "sleeping monster".

Skyscraper City:
http://www.skyscrapercity.com/forumdisplay.php?f=671

The architecture blog has a long and ever-expanding section on architecture new and old in Athens.

Mikis Theodorakis: http://en.mikis-theodorakis.net/
The encyclopedic official site for the composer.

Triple Bath: http://www.triplebath.gr/
A more international flavour at this Athens-based indie label that also released Coti K's *Ondas*.

Savina Yannatou: http://www.savinayannatou.com/
Music, videos and more about the singer's work.

Iannis Xenakis: http://www.iannis-xenakis.org/
Site of the Friends of Xenakis Association, with an extensive archive, biographical details and sound excerpts.

Index